# FUTURE CHRIST

**Also available from Continuum:**

# FUTURE CHRIST
## A Lesson in Heresy

*François Laruelle*

*Translated by* Anthony Paul Smith

continuum

**Continuum International Publishing Group**

| | |
|---|---|
| The Tower Building | 80 Maiden Lane |
| 11 York Road | Suite 704 |
| London SE1 7NX | New York, NY 10038 |

www.continuumbooks.com

Originally published in French as *Le Christ futur* © Exils Éditeur, 2002. All rights reserved.

This authorized English language translation from the French edition © the Continuum International Publishing Group, 2010

**British Library Cataloguing-in-Publication Data**
A catalogue record for this book is available from the British Library.

ISBN: HB: 978-1-4411-1833-2    **1006278325**

**Library of Congress Cataloging-in-Publication Data**
Laruelle, François.
[Christ future. English]
Future Christ : a lesson in heresy / François Laruelle ; translated by Anthony Paul Smith.
    p. cm.
Includes bibliographical references and index.
ISBN 978-1-4411-1833-2
1. Jesus Christ–History of doctrines. 2. Heresy. I. Title.

BT1315.3.L3713 2010
232'.8–dc22

                                                    2010019822

Typeset by Newgen Imaging Systems Pvt Ltd, Chennai, India
Printed and bound in India by Replika Press Pvt Ltd

'Who were we, what have we become?
Where are we, whence are we being thrown?
From whither do we hasten, from what are we redeemed?'

Theodotus, *Excerpta Ex Theodoto*, §78*

---

* Translation modified to fit the French translation. Clement of Alexandria (2006), *Extraits de Théodote*, trans. François Sagnard, O.P. (Paris: Éditions de Cerf).

# Contents

# The Triptych: Author's Foreword

The Triptych is a set of three autonomous works, coordinated by the material of their themes and objects and unified by their practice of thought. The first panel (*Future Christ: A Lesson in Heresy*) is a heretical introduction to the two others. The central panel is a mystical one (*Théorèmes mystiques*). Lastly, an erotic conclusion (*Principia amoris, la science des amants*) groups or closes the altarpiece.[1]

The style of these works is mainly but not uniquely philosophico-religious. The first in particular is a manifesto on the 'heretic question' likened to the themes of the Shoah, according to its memory and forgetting, to history and the vanquished of history, persecution, etc. All come under a style I call 'theory' characterized by axioms and theorems known as 'transcendentals'. They experimentally shuffle around material from Christianity, gnosis, mysticism, erotic poetry, and lastly from philosophy. On the one hand they are distinguished from classic 'philosophy of Christianity' projects by method and object. They are treated in order to fashion the theory out of a field of phenomena each time reduced to some fundamental elements, Christianity and gnosis for the first, Christian mysticism for the second, and lastly amorous unions for the third. On the other hand they establish new real-life conditions, the same as the theoretical ones, which also has within it already a whiff of 'belief', 'mysticism', and 'lover', as it still is 'philosophy', and that which these terms mean for her.

This being the univocal theoretical schema that structures both this set of works and non-philosophy, a minimal glossary of non-philosophy is offered at the beginning as a glossary raisonné rather than an alphabetical dictionary. The two main difficulties to surmount are, on the one hand, the logic displayed, rebellious to philosophy and to Christianity with which it is constantly battling, and on the other hand what this logic allows here, extreme freedom from conceptual vocabularies, or as it were from 'arguments' utilized as variables in the same way. The glossary should familiarize the reader with the style of thought, provided that it is treated as an adaptive instrument depending on its material. Turning the glossary into a 'model' or 'system' closed in on itself would be contrary to the spirit of non-philosophy which is a practice of – and in – thought.

François Laruelle

## NOTE

[1]  As of the completion of this translation Laruelle has not completed all three volumes of his 'triptych'. The second was published in 2007 under a different title than the one given above as *Mystique non-philosophique à l'usage des contemporains* [*Non-Philosophical Mysticism for Contemporary Use*] (Paris: L'Harmattan). The third has yet to be published.

# The Philosopher and the Heretic: Translator's Introduction

## A STRANGER THOUGHT

You hold in your hands a strange, alien treatise. It is, as the reader will quickly see, strange in its vocabulary and syntax, though this is not in the name of some postmodern pastiche, intellectual cunning, or disregard for the reader, but rather an effort to think differently, to think as an alien of and for this World through a mutation of Worldly philosophical language. Strange in its content, for example, it directs our thinking on religious violence away from the usual locations that intellectuals traverse, the Holocaust of European Jews (the Shoah) or the Islamic suicide bomber, directing our attention instead to the murder of heretics, murder which Laruelle claims witnesses to something more universal – the murder of man as man or human beings as human beings. Strange too in its method, which Laruelle calls dualysis, freely constructing theories about religion, violence, memory, salvation, belief and time from out of the various dualisms that populate philosophical and theological thinking. It is strange also in the interest it takes in religion, neither aiming for a pietistic defence of or atheistic assault on religion, as one gets in much Anglophone philosophy of religion, nor is it just another variant of the 'turn to religion' that one finds in a variety of forms of contemporary European philosophy. It is strange because this is not a work of philosophy as such; it is a work of prolonged heresy, a heresy that is continuously heretical, never allowing itself to accept even that heresy is sufficient.

So what then is the reader to do with this strangeness? The answer is a simple, practical one, in fact the answer is the same as it is for every strange theory one encounters for the first time. The reader simply has to read and think alongside the text in its presentation, argumentation and development of a theory of non-Christianity and heresy. This introduction aims to provide the reader with some tools in that journey, helping to situate the book within the wider project of non-philosophy generally and where that project fits within the Contemporary landscape of both philosophy and theology/ religious thought as well as their liminal spaces. It does not aim to be a technical article, but a casual discussion about the particular practice of non-philosophy and the surrounding materials upon which it draws.

## A MINIMAL INTRODUCTION TO NON-PHILOSOPHY

The career of François Laruelle spans nearly fifty years, with his first book-length publication appearing in 1971. For nearly forty of those years he has turned his attention towards the development of the practice of non-philosophy. This book is, within that history, relatively recent, having originally been published in 2002, and the book draws on that long development. The first tool then that the reader will find helpful as they begin to read non-philosophy is a short history of that development. On the first few pages of a book, along with the title page and other material unrelated to the content of the book, you will often find a list of other books the author has written. Laruelle's list is slightly different than other philosophers' as his books are broken up into four periods, Philosophy I–IV. This periodization of his works corresponds to different phases in the development of non-philosophy. The first period of his work is not properly non-philosophical, marked as it is by a kind of rebellious apprenticeship in philosophy. During this period he wrote highly original secondary works of philosophy. Included in this period is the minor thesis on Félix Ravaisson that he submitted for his doctorate (during that time in France a student had to submit a major and minor thesis to be awarded the doctorate), a number of works deploying Nietzsche in a contemporary context, for instance in a study of Derrida's deconstruction and another on Heidegger's philosophy, and a book on political philosophy.

It is during this period that Laruelle discovered what he would come to call the 'Principle of Sufficient Philosophy'. The Principle of Sufficient Philosophy is the unacknowledged faith in philosophy that everything is philosophizable. An invariant founding gesture of philosophy as practised in the West that says we can construct a unitary philosophy *of* X, whether the X be religion, science, art, society, politics or even of philosophy itself, what we normally call metaphilosophy. Philosophy is able to master it all; it is able to take the identity of the variable and process it through the structure of philosophy in order to produce a mixture that allows the philosopher to confuse X with the philosophical structure itself.

Such a critique is not uncommon in contemporary European philosophy and it even shares aspects in common with Anglo-American pragmatism and analytic philosophy. The difference between philosophers from those traditions and Laruelle is that they go on to construct some new philosophy that will eliminate the errors of the previous philosophies. Laruelle, however, does not aim to construct a new philosophy; he aims for a heretical practice of questioning the identity of philosophy itself, and so in the period of non-philosophy he calls Philosophy II he breaks with the Principle of Sufficient Philosophy; he breaks with philosophy, in order to develop what he calls a science of philosophy. He does not, though, become a scientist, but rather becomes a heretic within the faith of philosophy. Crucially this science of philosophy is not an anti-philosophy, in the same way that heretics are never anti-Christian, anti-Jewish, anti-Islamic, or what have you, but are mutations of the so-called orthodox beliefs and practices. Though Laruelle is critical of the underlying philosophical faith he does not aim at the absolute destruction of philosophy, but at a new invention of philosophy. The aim is instead to use philosophy to construct new theories without those theories being determined by the Principle of Sufficient Philosophy: 'All is not philosophizable, this is my good news.'[2] In this way, Laruelle is able to bring peace to the philosophers, who wage total war on one another in their attempt to provide the final philosophy of everything, an all-philosophy or what he will call in this book 'the-philosophy'; a unitary conception of philosophy that operates as a hallucination of what philosophy is.

Laruelle thus makes an appeal to science, the same science that had for so long been judged by philosophers to 'not think', in order to subject philosophy to a scientific condition, to place the practice of philosophy in a scientific posture, to mutate it using scientific means related to the actual practice of science rather than the philosophical image of science and to a religious posture that posits a One beyond Being and Otherness; these two postures are brought together into a single one. Laruelle's appeal to science may strike the post-Heideggarian reader as particularly scientistic or, following either Foucault or Latour, a misguided idealization of what could be called following the style of this book 'the-Science'. This is not the case, and I will try to explain why. For Laruelle, much like for Badiou (a philosopher perhaps more familiar to us today), science should not be confused with the debasement of science within capitalism where science's power is confused with the power to create profit or wish for some unitary entity that is fully consistent and functioning within itself. Instead, science is here meant in a somewhat older sense as *theoria*, but also as knowledge that solves problems, that knows things through their use, through 'taking them in hand'. Philosophy II's appeal to science marks Laruelle's break with thinking under the conditions of philosophical hallucination, this philosophical (self-)sufficiency, but that break is, he tells us, 'more than a break or more than a new primary decision, it is the subordination of the non-philosophical decision to its immanent cause, the vision-in-One'.[3] Laruelle tells us quite simply in his *Dictionnaire de la non-philosophie* that 'The philosophical decision is an operation of transcendence that believes (in a naïve and hallucinatory way) in the possibility of a unitary discourse of the Real.'[4] In order to overcome the narcissism that arises out of the philosophical decision, where the philosopher ends up turning his X, some aspect of the Real, into a mirror of his philosophy in whose reflection he is caught, Laruelle situates the philosophical decision in its immanent cause – the vision-in-One. The vision-in-One is equivalent to the Real, meaning that when one thinks *from* (rather than *about*) the Real then one is thinking from the vision-in-One as radical immanence. Laruelle appears to be intentionally obscure about what the One *is*, its *being*, because non-philosophy aims to renounce the philosophical desire-for-the-One or the thought-of-the-One that always subordinates the One to Being.[5] One can, however, come to know from-the-One when one begins to realize that all discourses persist through the vision-in-One, but do not in themselves constitute *the* discourse on the One. The One is radical immanence itself and thus the vision-in-One is immanent to the One itself; it has an identity that is distinct from Being or Alterity. Thus Philosophy II was founded on two complimentary axioms: '1. The One is vision immanent in-One. 2. There is a special affinity between the vision-in-One and the phenomenal experience of "scientific thought".'[6]

If Philosophy II is where Laruelle first develops the scientific practice of non-philosophy, a vision-in-One, and confronts philosophy with science, then the shift from Philosophy II to III is subtler than the one that marks the move from Philosophy I to II. Laruelle came to regard the second axiom of Philosophy II, which stated that scientific thought had some privilege in thinking the Real via an affinity with the vision-in-One, as a mere reversal of the reigning post-Kantian epistemico-logical hierarchy. This reversal ultimately constituted a 'ruse of philosophy' that allowed it to refuse 'to surrender to the real'.[7] Philosophy III begins with the suspension of this second axiom of Philosophy II in order to begin thinking from the radical autonomy of the Real – not as a reversal of Philosophy II's valorization of science, but in order to free the Real from all authority, even that of science, now using science as a simple material alongside of philosophy in an equivalent manner. Laruelle summarizes the history up to this point, writing,

> If Philosophy I is intra-philosophical and if Philosophy II marked the discovery of the non-philosophical against philosophy and to the benefit of science, Philosophy III frees itself of the authority of science, in actuality from every hierarchical philosophical spirit, and takes as object the whole of philosophical sufficiency. It corresponds thus paradoxically to the self-affirmation of philosophy, but 'negatively' or finally for the suspension of it over all.[8]

Philosophy III is, then, the proper start of non-philosophy nearly freed from the vicious circle of the philosophical decision. It aims at the construction of 'unified theories' through a method of dualysis and a causality of determination-in-the-last-instance.

A unified theory is Laruelle's term for a non-philosophical practice of thought that replaces the formerly narcissistic philosophy of X. So, for instance, instead of a 'philosophy of religion' or a 'philosophy of science' one constructs, under these new non-philosophical axioms, a unified theory of philosophy and religion or a unified theory of philosophy of science. Unified, not unitary, because the theory is also only occasional, such that its axioms are well-founded but the practice of the theory is utterly dependent on the material available and revisable upon the availability of new material. In both cases the terms retain their identities, neither philosophy, religion, nor science is subsumed within the other, because the unified theory is constructed from the axiomatic causality of the One as determination-in-the-last-instance and the method of dualysis that thinks from that causality.

The determination-in-the-last-instance (or – identity, following the mutation it undergoes in *Future Christ*) is the tracing of the causality of the One in the vision-in-One; it traces the unilateral causal relationship between the Real-One and thought. Unilateral because the relationship only goes one way, thought cannot affect the Real-One, the Real-One is foreclosed to thought. This concept comes from Marxism, a notion propounded by Engels and reworked by Althusser, where it referred to the primacy or dominance of the economic over other aspects of human life. As understood by Althusser it was not that everything was simply economic, but that in the last instance economics was the dominant causal force in human life. Laruelle radicalizes this notion by subtracting it from the framework of historical materialism and setting it within a transcendental realist framework where the Real-One is what is unilaterally causal, without that then meaning that everything is simply reduced to it, but rather everything philosophy claims to master is in-the-last-instance thinkable *from* the One-Real.[9] This axiomatic description of the causal relationship of the Real-One to thought frees philosophy from the pretence that it can adequately think the Real, this is its condition of negative freedom, while at the same time freeing it to finally think adequately, that is non-philosophically, about the various aspects, we may even say *regions*, of reality that philosophy has concerned itself with, its condition of positive freedom.

The method for this way of thinking is called dualysis. The axiomatic causality of determination-in-the-last-instance is the ground of this method, because its foreclosing of the Real-One to thought allows us to take the various dualisms that populate philosophy as equivalent in their relationship to the Real-One. These dualisms are said by Laruelle to form a mixture of transcendence and immanence. This mixture allows for the terms to shift back and forth between one another, causing all sorts of confusions and allowing for the 'infinite task' of philosophy to continue, endlessly mixing and remixing the terms of its dualisms. By making the terms of these dualisms equivalent in their relationship to the Real-One, Laruelle separates the terms from their mixture, bestowing them with their identity within the philosophical structure. At various places he expresses this as a kind of formalism of the One.[10] The dualism, as a thought, is in unilateral causal relationship with the One where one aspect of the dualism, the one taking the place of transcendence, will correspond to a non (-One) while the other, taking the place of a relative philosophical immanence, will correspond to a (non-)One. The non(-One) indicates that the transcendent element of thought is a kind of negation, a hallucinatory aspect of thought that arises from the foreclosed nature of the Real-One. It is that aspect of thought that responds to the trauma of the foreclosing by negating the radical immanence of the One, reducing it to some hallucinatory transcendence of Being, Alterity, Difference, etc., but this aspect is at the same time *actually transcendent* within that philosophical occasion, but only as rooted in the radical immanence of the One.[11] While the (non-)One is the aspect of the dualism that corresponds to a relative immanence as found in philosophy, but this immanence is always corrupted by its relational convertibility with the term of transcendence and so the (non-)One indicates its mutation of the radical immanence of the One. Note that this separates him from both philosophies of transcendence and philosophies of immanence, as his is a non-philosophy from the radical immanence of the One, and it is this radical immanence that finally in the end forms the non-philosophical *unilateral* duality. After the identities of the dualisms terms have been separated out they are treated according to the causality of determination-in-the-last-instance, as a duality that is unilaterally determined from some first name of radical immanence, such as the Real-One. In simple terms, the two relative terms, non(-One) and (non-)One, have a real identity let us say X and Y, but from the perspective the Real-One there is a unilateral relation in the duality such that from the perspective of X there is both X and Y, but from the perspective of Y there is only Y because Y's identity includes X's identity.

## THE PHILOSOPHICAL HOMELESSNESS OF THE HERETIC

This brings us to the stage of non-philosophy which this book inaugurates, Philosophy IV. At this stage Laruelle has moved fully into the realm of unified theories. While in Philosophy III his construction via dualysis of a unified theory of philosophy and science still deals in large part with philosophical systems of thought, be it Cartesianism or Marxism, in Philosophy IV Laruelle turns his attention to material from within non-philosophical discourses like religion and science. It is these two non-philosophical discourses, often seen to be at odds with one another, that Laruelle has focused on in the period of Philosophy IV, making both answer to a human ultimatum. This is perhaps Laruelle at his most inventive, a non-philosophy that has finally broken fully with the Principle of Sufficient Philosophy, no longer even staring from a third position at the philosopher staring in the mirror, but putting the method of non-philosophy to use on a number of regional discourses that are also haunted by this structure of various forms of interplay between transcendence and relative immanence. It is easy when faced with a strident and far-reaching critique of all philosophy to lose oneself in the excitement brought about by the freedom the critique has given. Indeed, nearly all the existing English-language literature has focused on this criticism and, while this has already produced interesting work and debates, even pushing forward projects that reject the moniker non-philosophy, there is the fear that it can stagnate into a mere discussion of this freedom rather than its practice. To call to mind that English difference between negative and positive freedom, already hinted at above, the reader who has only discovered Laruelle's work via discussions around Speculative Realism could perhaps think that Laruelle provides us freedom *from* philosophy but *for* nothing. He has been grouped in with the deflationary metaphysics of eliminative materialism and alternatively with their opposite as a Heideggerian thinker in expectation that only a God can save us. It is in part this situation, where discussions of Laruelle were beginning to take place without any of his own works available to read in English, that lead me to translate *Future Christ*, as it is an example of the constructive aspect of his science of philosophy (what is mistakenly taken to be a mere critique) after his break with philosophical (self-)sufficiency. It is an example of the positive non-philosophical programme of heresy.

Where though does the non-philosophical heretic fit in within the wider contemporary philosophical scene? While Laruelle first came to the attention of Anglophone readers because of a remark made in Deleuze and Guattari's *What is Philosophy* (there they remark that 'François Laruelle is engaged in one of the most interesting undertakings of contemporary philosophy'[12]), it was the work of Ray Brassier that really introduced the reader to Laruelle's non-philosophy, first through his doctoral dissertation then through a series of articles in *Pli* and *Radical Philosophy* and finally in his popular work (by Continental philosophy standards) *Nihil Unbound: Enlightenment and Extinction* where he uses Laruelle as one piece in his own nihilistic philosophy.[13] Around the same time John Mullarkey began a study of Laruelle as one among four contemporary French philosophers concerned primarily with immanence.[14] Both provide excellent synthetic readings of Laruelle that are indispensible for the reader just beginning with non-philosophy. Mullarkey's study has the added benefit of placing Laruelle's thought within a comparative study of three major philosophers of immanence (Deleuze, Henry, Badiou), each of whom Laruelle draws upon in his various constructions of theory, but Mullarkey's synthetic and comparative reading simply has no place for what exactly Laruelle's work on religion means, it is not a central issue in his reading. For Mullarkey instead shows us that philosophies which reduce philosophy to either science (as the matheme in Badiou) or to religion (as the patheme in Henry) are themselves practising the very kind of philosophy that Laruelle seeks to break with. Already in the Anglophone literature we see that the heretic is homeless in the interminable war between philosophy working out of science and philosophy working out of religion.

Brassier too has no place for religion in his various presentations of non-philosophy and his own philosophy aims at a kind of disavowal of the compromised relationship European philosophy has with religion, specifically Judeo-Christian monotheism; this disavowal takes the form of a strong rationalist elimination of the religious from philosophical thought sutured to scientific truth. It is interesting that in his footnote screed against the temptation to the theological in European philosophy Brassier does not list Laruelle in either the 'avowed atheist' list of thinkers committed to scientific rationalism or the list of those contaminated by 'theological overtones'.[15] Brassier is surely aware of Laruelle's work on religion, as he quotes from other works in Philosophy IV that deal with religion, but Laruelle does not fit neatly into this separation of thinkers (which is true of several of the thinkers in both lists). Laruelle clearly draws on thinkers whose work is explicitly theological (like Henry) just as much as does from thinkers whose work is explicitly atheist-rationalist (like Badiou), but he makes his home with neither of them. Instead he subjects all forms of philosophy, including Christianity and those forms of unacknowledged philosophy that populate scientific thought, to a scientific condition and frees from the material of religion and science that which is of human use towards the construction of a future.

Religion remains of interest to Laruelle, even though he has set it under the same condition as philosophy before the Real (which is a scientific practice), because religion is equivalent before the Real and can be transformed by thinking it according-to-the-Real. This allows Laruelle to disentangle religion from the elements of religion that are clearly useful for human beings in the construction of a future. Laruelle's construction of a future non-Christianity is certainly not a friend to the pious Christian who reads his book attentively, but presents a heretical, strange thought to the Christian theologian who has ears to hear. It is bizarre then to read the Radical Orthodox/Red Tory theologian John Milbank making reference to this very book as if it supported his assertion about the supremacy of Christianity. He writes,

[. . .] the atheistic can seem curiously akin to the theological, and, in the case of Hegel, Badiou, Laruelle, and Žižek, it is forced to take even a Christological shape – Christ is the final, divine man, precisely because he elevates free personality beyond essence or even existence (also beyond law, physical and political, and beyond even the concealed founding axioms of philosophy that require a prior determination of the determinate) into an absolute, and exhibits this as fully present in his finite existence alone.[16]

It is not that Laruelle's non-philosophy is forced to take a Christological shape, but that he chooses as a heretic to work with that material and fashion something strange from it. For the dualysis of Christianity separates out God-World [non(-One)] and Future Christ as subject as the relatively immanent [(non-)One] that are in the end unilateralized from the radical immanence of Man-in-Man/Man-in-person as a privileged name of the Real. The heretic has no home, no World, but only his inalienable immanence as Man-in-person and that, as the cause of both science and religion, is enough salvation for the heretic and what he offers to the philosophers and theologians. He who has ears to hear . . .

## NOTE ON THE TRANSLATION

Laruelle's writing is renowned for its difficulty owing in part to his focus on syntax and the intentional attempt to make non-philosophy a stranger to the usual ways of thinking. There is a remarkable simplicity to his theory, but that simplicity is only discovered within a mutation of the usual philosophical language. Owing to Laruelle's focus on syntax I have tended towards a more literal translation than may be preferable, but if this means the translation loses something in the way of idiomatic English it is because it seemed necessary as it allowed me to retain the structure of the syntax more faithfully. I have kept translator's notes to a minimum focusing on a few neologisms and untranslatable sentences that required some explication. Note that there are no endnotes in the French original and so all notes are my own.

Laruelle draws freely on a remarkable number of conceptual vocabularies from across the history of philosophy and religion. I have tried to follow the accepted translations of these words (though I have not followed the usual translation of Levinas's *Autrui* as 'other', pre-ferring instead the more literal 'Other people'). I hope this will allow the text's resonances with these more familiar systems of thought to manifest for the reader. For example, I have followed the usual translation (following translations of French literature on Heidegger) of *Étre* and *étant* as 'Being' and 'beings' and the English translation 'foreclosed' for Lacan's concept of *forclusion*.

There are a number of conceptual terms that are found throughout Laruelle's work whose sense in English I have had to decide. I have translated *mélange* consistently as 'mixture' because of its resonances with Anglophone translations and scholarship on Gnostic texts, and have translated *mixte* as 'mix'. For *mondaine*, which in philosophical writing is usually translated as 'mundane', I have followed the more religious translation as 'worldly', as this resonates more with Laruelle's discussion of the World in the French between *Monde* and *mondaine*. Finally, the most difficult concept to translate in the whole book has been *Homme-en-personne*. Despite the discomfort the gendered term holds, especially as it is Laruelle's attempt to describe a 'generic' con-ception of a human being, I have translated the first part as 'Man' in the sense of species-being. The whole term can suggest a denouement of the human person as 'Man-in-no-one' or a kind of excess of Man as 'Man-in-anyone'. However, the first suggests a kind of nihilistic determination of Laruelle's non-philosophy that is lacking (though there may be within it occasions of nihilism that Laruelle uses just as he uses Christianity) and both translations would lose the sense of 'person' that is important for Laruelle's interaction with the Christian doctrine of the Trinity ('One God in three persons'). The option that appears to hold as much of the French would be a somewhat monstrous 'Man-in-any-person', so for the sake of economy I have translated it as 'Man-in-person'. The variance of meaning and the generic sense should be kept in mind when reading the phrase.

## ACKNOWLEDGEMENTS

This translation was completed during my third year of Ph.D. studies at the University of Nottingham in the Theology and Religious Studies

Department, but it would never have been completed without the University of Dundee's Department of Philosophy, a place whose support of my work and the friendship offered to me by its faculty and students made it something of a second academic home during my studies. Two Dundonians deserve particular recognition. First, the translation may have never been commissioned without the enthusiasm of John Mullarkey for Laruelle's work and his standing behind the proposal. Second, without the assistance of Nicola Rubczak the translation would be much poorer. She kindly looked over every line of the French and English and helped untangle a number of tangled sentences giving the translation a higher level of clarity and accuracy. They both have my highest gratitude for the gift of friendship they've shown during the process. Thanks also to Alberto Toscano, for his support, and to Ray Brassier whose off-hand remark in 2008 about the relative ease of reading and translating Laruelle's work convinced me to begin a study of non-philosophy (one which I doubt he even remembers making in the Dundee Contemporary Arts bar after a conference on philosophy after Deleuze, such are the contingences of intellectual projects). My appreciation goes to Adam Kotsko, Eleanor Andrews, Joshua Delpech-Ramey, Gabriel Rockhill and Rocco Gangle for taking time to help me with a number of sentences, and to Brad Johnson for reading through the introduction. All remaining errors, of course, are my own. Philip Goodchild, my doctoral supervisor, also deserves my gratitude for supporting this undertaking while working on my dissertation and for the continued intellectual inspiration he provides me. My utmost thanks to the editorial team at Continuum, Sarah Campbell, who originally commissioned the translation, David Avital, who carried on the work when Sarah went on leave, and Tom Crick, who did much of the legwork for the book's preparation. Continuum deserves praise for being brave and far-sighted enough to finally bring the stimulating, wild and free work of François Laruelle to Anglophone readers. Finally, thank you to François Laruelle who has practised the utmost kindness and patience towards me while exploring his work. He has practised a kind of ultimatum of friendship towards me, always open to questioning and explanation, without regard for any of the usual academic hierarchies. I hope he accepts this translation of his work as a small token of my gratitude for that kindness.

## NOTES

1   The history I provide here is constructed in part using the history Laruelle himself provides in his important *Principes de la non-philosophie*. See F. Laruelle (1996), *Principes de la non-philosophie* (Paris: PUF), pp. 38–42.

2   F. Laruelle (1991), *En tant qu'Un: La « non-philosophie » expliquée aux philosophes* (Paris: Aubier), p. 246. [All translations are mine unless noted.]

3   Laruelle (1995), p. 31.

4   F. Laruelle (ed.) (1998), *Dictionnaire de la non-philosophie* (Paris: Éditions Kimé), p. 40. See also Taylor Adkins draft translation of this passage and the rest of the *Dictionnaire* available online: <http://nsrnicek.googlepages.com/DictionaryNonPhilosophy.pdf>. My own translation is modified from that of Adkins.

5   See the entry 'Vision-en-Un (Un, Un-en-Un, Réel)' in Laruelle (1998), pp. 202–205.

6   Laruelle (1995), p. 39.

7   Ibid.

8   Laruelle (1995), p. 40.

9   See Laruelle (1998), pp. 48–52.

10  See Laruelle (1986), *Les Philosophies de la différence. Introduction critique* (Paris: PUF), pp. 237–240.

11  See Laruelle (1986), pp. 215–219.

12  Gilles Deleuze and Félix Guattari (1994), *What is Philosophy*, trans. Hugh Tomlinson and Graham Burchell (New York: Columbia University Press), p. 220, footnote 5.

13  See R. Brassier (2001). 'Behold the Non-Rabbit. Kant, Quine, Laruelle', *Pli: The Warwick Journal of Philosophy*, 12, 50–82. R. Brassier (2003), 'Axiomatic Heresy: The Non-Philosophy of François Laruelle', *Radical Philosophy*, 121, 24–35. R. Brassier (2007), *Nihil Unbound: Enlightenment and Extinction* (Basingstoke: Palgrave Macmillan), pp. 118–149.

14  See J. Mullarkey (2006), *Post-Continental Philosophy: An Outline* (London and New York: Continuum), pp. 125–156.

[15]  Brassier (2007), p. 246 footnote 13.

[16]  J. Milbank (2009), 'The Double Glory, or Paradox versus Dialectic: On Not Quite Agreeing with Slavoj Žižek' in *The Monstrosity of Christ: Paradox or Dialectic?*, ed. Creston Davis (Cambridge, MA and London: MIT Press), pp. 154–155.

# Glossary Raisonné: Rules for Writing Non-Philosophy (Vocabulary and Syntax)

## GENERAL FORMATION OF FIRST NAMES

*First names*

Fundamental terms which symbolize the Real and its modes according to its radical immanence or its identity. They are deprived of their philosophical sense and become, via axiomatized abstraction, the terms – axioms and theorems – of non-philosophy.

*Material (of non-philosophy)*

Concepts from philosophy and its sub-disciplines (theology, mysticism, etc.) that serve as support-terms for the first names. The material constitutes a philosophical situation that is different each time.

*Axiomatized abstraction*

Proceeds by way of operators from names (like One, Identity or Man), from adjectives like radical (radical identity, etc.), from prepositions like in- (One-in-One, etc.), without (without-consistency, without-world, etc.), non- (non-conceptual, non-definitional, etc.), in-person (Man-in-person, One-in-person, etc.). These operators are the expression and the effects of the Real, which are inseparable from its radical immanence.

FIRST NAMES FOR THE REAL

*Real*

General first name for that which is separated from the World by its immanence and able to determine it in-the-last-identity.

*Immanence*

Immanence is not an attribute without also being the subject, it is by definition given in-immanence, as the Real is given in-Real, it is the essence of the in-, of the radical, of the Real, etc.

*One*

An ancient transcendental utilized as a first name under the forms One-in-One, One-in-person, vision-in-One.

*Identity*

Real identity or through immanence, not logical or determined by a principle, the Principle of Identity.

*Man-in-person, Man-in-Man, Humans*

Other first names for the Real, Immanence, One or Identity that cease to be anonymous transcendentals and indicate the reduction which makes them human. One may say the human Real, the human Identity, but human is also a name, Human Beings and the Humane.

FIRST NAMES FOR PHILOSOPHY

*1. Vocabulary*

*Philosophy*
Instance (and its sub-groups, here Christianity, gnosis, sect, heretical-religious) opposed to the Real in the mode of a symptom and bound to undergo its causality.

*Philosophical decision*
Transvariant structure, system-shaped, that combines dyad and triad, indeterminate if it is set down by philosophy itself (The-Philosophy), or determinate if it is set within non-philosophy according to the Real. It is then the non-philosophical Identity (of) for philosophy.

*World*
Other name for philosophy under its two forms. Philosophy is world-shaped, the World is thought-world.

*2. Syntax*

*Sufficiency (principle of sufficient philosophy)*
Pretension of philosophy to co-determine the Real or Man who is foreclosed for it.

*Auto-inclusion*
Cause of sufficiency, philosophy being divided or redoubled in each of its concepts and forming an auto-position or a transcendental vicious circle.

*The-philosophy*
A composition, by aggregation of a term and its article, from either the common and vague notion or from the philosophical notion about a field of phenomena (the-gnosis, the-Christianity, the-world, etc.), or on the contrary from the transcendental identity or the clone of these notions (the vision-in-One, One-in-One, Man-in-Man, the-philosophy, etc.).

*World*
A composition by addition of the suffix '–world' to the term in question (God-world, Christ-world, etc.) indicates a sense of sufficiency.

FIRST NAMES FOR NON-PHILOSOPHY

*1. Names for philosophy*

All the preceding names are already in non-philosophical usage.

*2. Specific names for the causality of the Real (Real-in-person, Identity-in-person, Man-in-person, etc.).*

*Determination-in-the-last-identity*
Set of phases (cf. occasionality and cloning) regarding non-philosophical causality that are entirely opposed to the reciprocal or circular causality of philosophy and to its limited unilateral modes.

*Negative condition*
Of the Real qua necessary cause, but not sufficient or requiring the World to determine it. The Real, 'negative' cause, supposes the World in order to act.

*Given-without-givenness*
Essence of the manifestation of the immanent Real, and therefore also of the World.

*Unilaterality*
Duality of non-philosophical causality. The support or material of its effect is presented (abstracted from its auto-representation), but its cause is non-present or immanent in-One, without being absent.

*Clone*
Immanent identity of the philosophical material or symptom. Cloning is the work of the Real, it has philosophy or the World for material, it is an immanent and transcendental operation on the World's transcendence and substitutes itself for the philosophical system.

*Symptom*
Function of philosophy in non-philosophy when, its sufficiency immediately reduced from its being-in-Real or in-Identity, it is given

in the state of hallucinatory pretension about the Real and illusory about the subject.

*Dualysis*
General method of non-philosophy carried out on the philosophical material and which distinguishes itself from analysis, from synthesis and from their combinations (dialectic, difference). A practice which treats the world-terms according to a unilateral duality, introducing the determination-in-the-last-identity to it.

## 3. Names for the subject of non-philosophy

*Subject*
Other name for the clone. A unilaterally distinct instance of Man-in-person. It is the effect of determination-in-the-last-identity, that is, a function of the situation-symptom under the invariance of the Real.

*Stranger-subject, Christ-subject, Future Christ*
Modalities of the subject according to the philosophical (or other) situation chosen as material.

# CHAPTER ONE
## Future Christianity

FUNDAMENTAL CONCEPTS OF NON-CHRISTIAN SCIENCE

What illusion or what ruse . . . Is this not the 'Why?' of the victim which, already being the response, expects nothing to come from its desperate question, questions that are infantile in the measure of that expectation. 'What is philosophy?', 'What is the World?', or even 'What is Christianity?' are among the most infantile and the most clever as they create hope for a promise to come instead of making the declaration of, *in-the-last-response, Man-as-Future-Christ*. Christian practice, with naivety or cunning, evidently avoids these questions – either hesitating to pose them, as is the case for the most faint-hearted, or it knows the futility, as is the case for the most cunning. Both end by closing their eyes so that they cannot see or to make it seem as if they have seen . . . A traditional trick [*manège*] divides it. Under these armed theological forms it has remained within the order of a theoretical spontaneism lacking vigour or radicality and in the tow of philosophy as the least sought-after dogma. Inversely, the opposite claim, that of the 'living witness of faith' and the combination of faith and works in the world, takes pride in an absence of impression-istic, but distressing, thought. That which auto-proclaims itself 'the-Christianity', will it not be the one of Christians then? Even if the God of the philosophers and the learned is perhaps not the God of faith, it may still be that the theology of the theologians is not that of . . . the *non-theologians* and *non-Christians* that we would like to be. Which, despite appearances, would already be a minor tautology.

## FUTURE CHRIST

We delimit an *immanent struggle* for a Christianity that is evidently not very 'Christian', which is to say that it is a theoretical practice rather than a doctrine or dogma. A heretical struggle as rebellion, rather than as agonistic or reciprocal combat because this presupposes Combat itself as the true victor. We are pursuing an initial goal, indeed if we have one other than that of the immanence-without-goal of the struggle. It is solving the Gnostic problem of rebellion as priority of struggle over war and over every other determination of a theological nature. However, this solution continuously relies on Christianity, gnosis and more distantly on Marxism, but refuses the Greek confusion of struggle with the agonistic that still marks rebellion. The notions pulled from these formations of knowledge are indications and symptoms for a theory, rather than for a dogmatic or apologetic position of this problem. To summarize the enterprise of first names as follows – *struggle is the essence of the subject, not of man, which it is not, in its immanence, 'in-struggle' and it is for that reason that we call it 'Man-in-person'.* And by the following theorem – *because there is a real cause of struggle that is not itself in-struggle – Man-in-person as radical identity – there is a subject-in-struggle.* 'The-man' of the philosophers and of common sense is a generality that levels out a special duality, an *indivi-duality* through which it is a cause or determinate identity of the subject in-struggle with the World, Christianity, gnosis and Judaism included. What is there at the beginning? The Act or the Word, the East or the West, the dawn of knowledge or barbaric darkness? In the beginning there is Struggle but Man-in-person is already another thing than that essence of the subject. He is determination-in-the-last-identity of struggle and, as such, he is not at the beginning, no more than at the end, of history. Man-in-person is neither above his beginning nor above his end. The subject alone, that which we call 'Future Christ', ceases not to begin or end in the immanence of its beginning, but it is not the holder of that immanence, it is only a function of the World under the condition of that immanence. It is by the elimination of 'human nature' and its 'real essences' that one has attempted to unitarily include men in 'humanity' and in some other fetishes, in the World. The title *Future Christ* demands a correct comprehension of its ultimate future character. And certain distinctions on the style of relations of struggle that are here possible. For example 'position' and 'partition' are fundamental concepts for thought, and 'party' and 'taking a stand' [*prise de parti*] are such for political struggle; all are usable here. Assume here then some variation of these terms or another distribution of their sense. In a very schematic way we are going to distinguish three postures:

1. The *'party* of Christianity' or easily, under that confession, of 'the-religion' that gathers together the adherents and the devout of a faith and its dogmas under the authority of the 'Principle of Sufficient Church', a principle that divides its practical and dogmatic spontaneism, its clumsy identifications, from heretical effervescence.

2. *Taking a position* that is religious or confessional, taking a position in 'the-Christianity' institutionalized as World, and that assumes therefore already the unitary horizon or the auto-inclusion of a sufficient religion and a sufficient church.

3. *Taking a stand* for Christianity, *for . . .* and not *in*. This conjugates a practice, a theory, and a pragmatic position designed to make universality and *radical* identities work, in this case from out of Christianity (as non-Christianity) and elsewhere from out of 'the-faith' and many more than from out of 'the-church' and its theology. Against the illusions and appearances of 'the-religion', against its fetishism and *for* other possibilities of use still unexpected from Christianity.

These distinctions of posture are without a doubt too simple, they are not at all empirical but transcendental and pertinent *for* the suppressed historico-religious. They are at least able to avoid a little of the bad faith that belongs to 'the-faith'.

But we are pursuing a second objective. For it is also, rather than a formal theoretical exercise, a matter of putting to the test what we call 'non-philosophy' within the field of phenomena that is religious (Christian, Judaic and Gnostic) and of planning a *heretical or non-Christian science* distinct from historical Christianity and religion in general. In a constant manner it refers there, however, to the point of claiming not to finally achieve it but explaining, from new (real and transcendental) grounds, that to which ancient Christian science aspired. In the same way that non-philosophy is no more, in the style of its Contemporaries, a margin of philosophy but the subject or organon that can think it and live it, the heresy of the Future Christ is no more a historical wandering to the limits of Christianity, sometimes unsympathetic to its dogmatics, a margin more or less rebellious to a church and, in particular, to the *catholica*. Rather, it is the outline of an organon that renders the religious-Christian phenomenon theoretically intelligible and lived humanly. It must be capable of explaining it in a 'transcendental' manner in an evidentially new sense, and certainly not in an empirical, historical or religious manner. Not a philosophy of Christianity as the nineteenth century has given the image of, perhaps for the ages, but the outline of a *non-philosophy for . . . Christianity*. That said, how does one distinguish the catholicity and the universality within the practice of Christianity? How does one not simply parody Nietzsche? Heresies, hearing one of them pretending to be the only and unique catholic church, die laughing. From laughing and not only from suffering . . .

INTRODUCING STRUGGLE-AS-PRIMARY:
*AGON*, REBELLION, AND STRUGGLE

We are right to make war, this is the thesis of the philosophers; to rebel against the master, this is the watchword of the Gnostics; to struggle in an immanent way with the World, this is the theorem of the Future Christ. In the beginning was the struggle, and the struggle was *with* the World and the World did not know it . . .

That is rebellion, its reasons and cause. Is that to say that the reasons for rebelling, which are by any measure precisely when it is *absolute* and *sufficient*, exhaust the cause of rebellion? What is more hopeless than a *Principle of Sufficient Rebellion*. One would not imagine an order so complete, with all the perfections of conformity, philosophical and worldly [*mondain*], that it included rebellion, expect perhaps class struggle. However, suffering and alienation, exclusion and crime, 'evil', are some *good* reasons. Reason itself is good, but does the excellence of the reasons and the motives explain the ultimate reality of rebellion? The only universally good rebellion and so already different than good, simply *real unlike good will*, is the rebellion of the '(immanent) because', but not 'because of . . .'. What will be a cause-without-reason except that which, being only from immanence or from identity, could determine one of them or transform the reasons advanced? Rebellion will be primary but less so than its cause which, in reality, does not have to be primary, even hyperbolically, being something other than a metaphysical cause.

We thus pose the decisive question to gnosis rather than to dominant Christianity, to Marxism rather than to philosophy, in front of this question they are cleared only because they have tried to respond to it: *what is the real cause of human struggle?* History is full of programmes of struggle (against the World, Capitalism and Globalization, Domination, the Master, Illusion, etc.). They are justified by oppression, servitude and exploitation, the transcendental appearance, evil, suffering, etc., but we ask if there is a *universal* struggle against all these evils, which does not justify their existence and takes them only as opportunities and circumstances? These programmes invented mediators, saviours, guides and avant-gardes, but we ask if there is a strictly human struggle which does not exhaust itself in empirical or philosophical, regional and fundamental motives? They inscribe themselves in the flow of history, in the immanence of economic production, in all kinds of exploitative trials, but we are looking for a struggle that cuts across history and the course of the World at a 'right angle', that maintains in flux the minimal relationship that Man-in-person maintains *in extremis* with the World before 'giving up', breaking off, or even allowing alienation of himself. This is a relation of struggle that is not backwards and the consequence of too much obvious exploitation of man by man, but one that exceeds the vicious circle and is determined by an inalienable nature or 'in-person' of man. A necessary struggle because it is not founded on alienation, to which Marxism and gnosis still partially subscribe, and that finds its real cause justified in the inalienable essence of Man-in-person. That this man is inalienable in-the-last-identity is not excluded, on the contrary he leads a struggle 'eternal and without hope' against an evil that is not philosophically identified and that he does not identify as such in the immanence of struggle, as its existence becomes confused purely with these, so he is the only living being which is defined, as subject, by struggle rather than by the discourse of Being or the Unconscious.

In order to clarify the stakes and the limits of rebellion we pose the problem outside of philosophical bad habits. Philosophy is always indifferent to man or, though this isn't very different, too quickly compassionate. Sufferings and alienation exist in the necessity of revolt and one concludes from this that there is evil, and often evils, there too. Revolts are only 'logical' in this way – admirable vicious circle of uncertainty and the contingency of a *desired rebellion* in which no one believes. We suppose an instant, or a time in history, another approach, in order to create a completely different hypothesis even if it seems at first to imitate the first one formulated here. *There is revolt rather than only evil*; nearly everywhere and always people do not cease to kill but they also rebel against the most violent powers as the most gentle. Starting from universal rebellion rather than from contingent reasons for rebelling (unfathomable and all too evident). What is the cause not of this revolt, but of this continuous power of revolt? It is already a fragile inference and completely contingent as the first hypothesis, but it is very interesting, very universal. It is always about passing from a diverse law to a necessary law of revolt, even if the contingency of the initial event leads to that conclusion. A philosophy of radical evil is always possible, but it seems impossible to make evil an *a priori* of our experience of the World, whereas rebellion may be, without damage, elevated to the level of *a priori* form of our relationship to the World. If evil is cruel then it immediately entails, in a reflexive way, rebelling precisely as a simple reaction of protection by which the intelligence of its cause is refused. It breaks immediately through thought and shackles itself in a vicious circle, erasing itself in the reaction where it fades away. Revolt, on the contrary, once considered as *a priori* irreducible to the phenomena of evil and suffering, compels and provokes thought to look outside of itself for a cause that is not exhausted in simply tracing its rationale from evil. *Why revolt and struggle instead of fleeing evil and its aggressions*? Or it would be necessary to admit that evil is more profound than aggression that leads to a reflexive reaction and that it affects the essence of man and is a direct menace to it, but it is not certain that philosophy is authorized or capable of giving meaning to this situation. The important distinction is not so much between that of evil and revolt but between revolt and defensive reflex. The latter is always as an auto-defence or protection because one cannot in this case defend oneself against the Other. Evil calls forth auto-defence in a privileged manner as a circle that thought cannot leave or into which it cannot enter. *How to make of rebellion something other than a reaction of auto-protection against aggression?* That is our question.

From this point of view one will always have thought struggle to be something secondary, where it occurs following an attack, but also, we have not examined that obvious symmetrical case, following a will to conquest and thus to auto-conquest, that never gives it the reality of an essence, the relative autonomy of a revolt in relation, without doubt, but not in a determinate way, with some oppression or some domination. One struggles in order to conquer or to defend oneself as if the essence of the subject had been to anticipate or even to react. Although founded upon a phenomenological or symbolic distance from the hunted or the aggressor, it is still an 'animal' essence there. Anticipating in preparation for conquest or reacting in preparation for defence, this is perhaps only a Greek vision of man, modelled from the anticipation-delay that is the distinctive essence of the metastable act of the philosopher. Between the heroic and athletic philosopher and the designated victim, we have never had the possibility of imagining another solution. Active or reactive, strong or weak, in spite of his effort to conceive their relationship in an immanent way, this is the horrible dilemma that Nietzsche preserved as an *inclusive* disjunction since the *affirmative* will to power had already settled the problem in a super-anticipatory way to the advantage of its *sufficiency*. 'Defend the strong against the weak': what humanely rigorous meaning could this abysmal formula have since it is already the strong and the victorious who pose the problem and choose the terms of the struggle?[1] The most profound difference is between struggle as rebellion and struggle as *agon*, which is a reflex either of conquest or of defence. Philosophy always thinks struggle, from the Greeks to Nietzsche and beyond, as agonistic rather than as rebellion. Elsewhere, from the Gnostics, it may conversely be that a rebellion is thought *as such*, but this too is already an *a posteriori* defence or reaction against the World or evil, which religious minds have opposed to the heroism of philosophical conquest, but without sufficiently displacing the terms of the problem.

How to understand rebellion as struggle so that it is no longer a philosophical reaction or reflection, as *the radical identity of a struggle in two unilateral aspects, against the World and for the World*? The first condition is that we make a struggle against philosophy and for it, since the World has a philosophical form. The second is that we subordinate the question of rebellion to that of struggle, because the first is immediately too directed against the World whereas the second, in its indetermination, is also properly more *against* . . . than *for*. . . The third, and most important, reduces the against and the for to the condition of aspects of a duality, but unilateral (from only one side) which they form with their unrepresentable human cause. This is in contradistinction to auto-defence and auto-mastery, and the other acts of philosophical narcissism, which turn into vicious circles. Sufficient or not or even partially insufficient, reasons and their greatest master, Reason, are given in the reciprocal petition of passivity and activity. They are set in a hyperbolic system, sometimes by the one (passivity of passivity, at the very worst; passivity more passive than all passivity, at best) and sometimes by the other (cause of self, will of will). The critical analysis of power, the innumerable political doctrines – of the State, of sovereignty – we know are among the exquisite pleasures where philosophy reassures itself of its existence and its usefulness. Philosophy would be more credible if it *considerably* extended that analysis to itself and, among other things, to Reason as auto-conquest and auto-defence which integrates all possible differences. From that point of view political philosophy conceals an apology of rational auto-defence that is more acceptable than that of auto-conquest but hardly more scientifically rigorous than it is humanly so. Rational auto-defence is theoretically sterile and practically it can only increase malaise and evil, thus increasing the injustice of the World.

It is not the question therefore of 'Who has begun, who takes the initiative, the capitalist or the proletariat?' that guides us. Are alienation and exploitation primary, against which it is necessary to defend oneself legitimately, meaning rationally, in preparation to create a new law? Or is this the Promethean task of the proletariat, representative of humanity, producers of capital, auto-alienated in this act? It is the revolt that commences and does not cease to commence in each instant, proletariat or not, exploitation or not. But if it has in itself sufficient reasons to start, it has only too many of them and cannot make a cause of them. Therefore *it must here have a cause which acts in revolt or in rebellion; these do not determine the cause but it determines them precisely as something other than auto-defence and a reaction linking them to the course of history and the course of the World, a cause which is in fact an autonomous struggle, against and for philosophy or the World in-person.* Two distinct operations are necessary so that revolt does not exhaust itself in the world (and not only in history). First, without doubt consider it as an *a priori* form of our relationship to the World (history included). But that form can not be *a priori* for the World itself and not only for its events or its objects, even if it is determined in being that form-for . . . , with that universal validity of an *a priori*, and not only an inference obtained by an empirico-philosophical induction which gives it no universal theoretical value. There it is the function of that cause, that the World does not know and which we are seeking, for rebellion in so much that it is not in the World, but that it acts, if it acts, for the World. It must be as if it is sufficiently separated from the World, owing it nothing for its reality and no longer obeying the Principle of Sufficient Rebellion, but as such so that it can transcendentally determine that rebellion-form in a way that is obviously not the old philosophical transcendental. This is the only way of proceeding which protects us, without being an auto-defence, from the fantasies of an absolute and purely religious rebellion.

'The-man' is a unitary, and not only gregarious, generality. *Dasein* does not break with this philosophical characteristic any more. Non-philosophy organizes it according to a 'unilateral duality', that of Man-in-person whose content is the vision-in-One (the inalienable Real) and of the subject as existing in-struggle or even as Stranger. The human is therefore without-Being (or without-World) but it determines-in-the-last-identity the subject-in-struggle with that which, from Being or from the World, can alienate it. If the subject finds in history the motives for revolt and the reasons for rebellion, it cannot exploit them as occasional causes and it is by these occasions that it constitutes itself as subject. But it returns to its being-exploited as soon as it supposes them sufficient for determining its battle and considers itself as an artefact of the World in order to finally annul and dissolve itself in it. Marxism attempts to explain struggle as class-struggle, programmed in spite of everything by its dialectical co-determination by the classes, and legitimating it by a cause more real than the idealist dialectic, but always standing solidly behind it since it is materialist. Gnosis subordinates rebellion to salvation through knowledge [*connaissance*], but it continues to understand this from the Greek-theoreticist mode and motivates rebellion by a religious conception of evil, enclosing evil and salvation in a mythical and philosophical circle. The identity of struggle, its autonomy, relative (to the World) but radical (by its cause), is destroyed in these concepts that, though more profound than those of philosophy, are nevertheless always unitary and auto-dissolving – without the knowledge, already giving one a reason to struggle (consequently idealist and theoreticist), of a transcendence. The source of the appearance is in the co-belonging of reason and revolt, *we evidently are right to revolt, rebellion has a reason – and why not a sufficient reason*? For historical gnosis, heaven has its reasons and maybe it even already has Greek reason, the specular theoreticism of all transcendence, for it. In order to be irreducible to the course of the World but 'tuned into' it, struggle needs a real cause, never a foundation, from an ontology of revolution or a transcendental ontology of rebellion. *There is rebellion and it is inextinguishable by suppression; there is struggle and it is insoluble in history and exploitation.* What is the cause that determines the subject as non-conformist, a cause in order not to enter into conformity with the Principle of Reason? Only Man-in-Man can exist, in his immanence, in the mode of struggle and discovery with his adversary, Grand Conformism.

Rebellion becomes rigorous when it ceases to be unitary and pure reaction, which is absolute even in a dialectical mode. Gnosis, which we will nonetheless elicit much from, has not gone past resentment, damning the World and understanding it as evil of the first order. 'Dualysing' [*Dualyser*] rebellion rather than analysing it, is setting it in a unilateral duality with the World as it is separated, it is giving it a cause that is not more sufficient, only necessary, and inscribing it, *under this condition of its being-separated*, in the string of intra-worldly struggles that must borrow their ways and motivations in order, in the same movement, to determine them according to Man-in-the-final-identity. These all-too-logical revolts are still revolution, class struggle and even Gnostic rebellion, searching for their ultimate justification in a modified form of the Logos (the absolute One, the dialectic, knowledge [*connaissance*] and its Greek primacy), but the struggle that finds its necessary but not sufficient cause in Man-in-person is a unilateral duality of phases rather than a unitary process.

Rather than the unity of a multiplicity of revolts or a comprehensive condemnation, rebellion must, in order to be effective, be the duality of a struggle proceeding in double (religious and philosophical, combining faith from one and from the other transcending) and from its determination as real or human-in-the-final-identity. It can only receive its sense of self by a sort of auto-negation or even from an auto-affirmation. There are two ways into the most radical struggles. One way is tuning directly into the World, an inventive and practical way because it equally includes heterogeneous procedures of struggle drawn from the World and turned against it (Christian faith and love, Gnostic refusal). And the other way, which is no longer really one, strictly speaking, is the vision-in-One of that struggle which is determined by Man who gives himself his reality and prevents it from returning to him, as to his self-sufficiency. When it is thus dual, but from a unilateral duality – a phase of struggle and one which is no longer of revolt but of human determination of revolt – it escapes from sufficient reason and makes itself a struggle-of-the-Stranger against . . . and for. . . the World according to a considered measure. We gain in this way from the most innovative practical part of Gnostic rebellion as well as from class struggle in order to gather with faith as so many simple *aspects* in the figure of Future Christ as subject-in-struggle.

TERROR AND THEORY

Non-philosophy is inseparable from the philosophical situation and, as here, from religion with its modalities and its derivatives, including sects and fanaticism, marked by war and religiously motivated terrorism. A problem all the more crucial since the most lively part of philosophy has already gone through these problems of rebellion, at best, and terror, at worst. Leaving aside the pacifist criticism of intellectuals who refused to go and see what philosophy brooded over in its depths. It is torn, in an example of turning to the extremes, between a Gnostic ideal (which can only be of interest to us) of rebellion as a total spiritual war against this World and its culture, and a Nietzschean or absolutely philosophical ideal (which can no longer leave us indifferent), an ideal softening of war soured in cruelty. 'Theory' in its ambiguity has become in the twentieth century the site of that very issue and that division. From the Gnostic side *theoricism* against culture and from the Nietzschean side the denunciation of terrorism and the blending of all-philosophy, as opinion that has become interesting or singular, together with the World more generally or, in other words: a form of capitalism. We place these two sides together under the sign of *theoreticism*, element and source of philosophy. It will be necessary to define this.

What remains to be said here, from non-philosophy, about the appearance of its struggle, in the militant name of 'theory', against a seemingly vague and global adversary, that is against 'the World' which it is quite prepared to call Evil-in-person? In order to shed light on these all too evident misunderstandings, hopeless moreover to remove them, it is necessary to go on a very long search within philosophy and from there onwards to religion for the bad rationale which creates a terrorist situation, in order to distinguish that which belongs to the actuality of the World and the radicality of the *Future Christ* in the appearance of violence. These roots are deeply hidden in the most secret mechanism of philosophy, a simple geostrategic or geophilosophical examination of the situation will not be enough to resolve this problem touching the essence of philosophy and religion. In order to catch sight of it, the most radical ways of non-philosophy are necessary, not only that of its object, philosophy, that conceals its possibility under a jumble of objects and all-too-honourable intentions. . .

What is theoreticism when it is taken as the final rendering of philosophy in its Greek origins? It is the nihilism of specular purity characteristic of transcendence that, by definition, splits and reflects itself in itself. It is the fundamental philosophical mechanism of Auto-position or Auto-transcendence. Theoreticism is not a deviation, except when taken in a restricted sense as in certain idealistically expressed doctrines, it is the specular essence of philosophy that confuses the *worthless* reflection of itself, itself as an absolute reflection without anything reflected, with the Real or Absolute. However the specular, whether it speculates or not and before being war and rivalry between men and between theories, is the element of terror imposing a reign of reflection as absolute void and empirical nothingness – the destruction of man. Affective tonality is more profound than the anxiety that discovers being. Perhaps terror is, for philosophy, ante-affective and fosters symptoms in philosophy under the forms of ontological wonder, sceptical doubt, anxiety, critique, and lastly in the ideologies of the 'blank slate'.

Terror has several futures [*destins*]. It is the ground of destruction, secret and silent, from where all wars are born *and which must be civilised precisely through a war or a philosophy. War and philosophy give birth to terror when terror is filled up and dispersed, as well as dominated, by objects and intentions of all sorts that fill it in and conceal it. It is the function of war and philosophy to tame terror and to form and codify it, to establish it within identifiable figures.* Without abolishing these, they soften theoreticism by way of 'theory' as a doctrine in the philosophical sense and by setting rules for war. But theory becomes *terrorism* when a religion or a policy seizes it and takes it in hand under conditions of a transcendence which are too radical for the auto-including nature and closure of philosophy and war, thus being conditions that philosophy and war exclude, preferring as they do mixed and measured skills to the logic of purity, purism and purification. How does violence speak so profoundly 'blind' to terrorism; could it be perhaps the depraved sister of theoreticism that would have to bring lucidity into the World? Terror is *a blind, auto-suppressed violence* which sees nothing because it has nothing to see. That blindness is the effect of the specular-whole, of the excess of the visible which shows nothing more, where even the light is night being unable to reflect itself upon any object. Terrorism and theoreticism are of the same family, in reality from the same cousinhood and known from the same family quarrels. But theory is something different, if it is not just theoreticism misunderstanding it or philosophically understanding it and believing it can be turned into a mode of terror, *therrorism* (Deleuze and Foucault).

Two reasons, in reality identical, exclude Greek *theoreticism* from non-philosophy. First, we claim for non-philosophy the force of 'theory', which has another sense than that of theoreticism. Is it an ultimate knowledge [*savoir*] but that we call 'unlearned knowledge' [*savoir indocte*] or vision-in-One in order to distinguish it not only from *docta ignorantia* [learned ignorance] (Nicholas of Cusa) but, by its radical immanence, from all knowledge taught and displayed from transcendence – that it is from the order of consciousness, the symbolic, or faith. Inevitable that such an untaught knowledge is confused, by philosophical transcendence, with the terror and its offspring of bad idealism. It is the great misunderstanding, the confusion of terror and rigour, of the blank slate with the untaught, of mad fantasy with the non-consistency of the Real, of blindness from an excess of light and of a blind knowledge that will not have been blinded.

Non-philosophy is moreover a *practice* of struggle under the form already known as unilateral duality. This excludes in any case the dialectic, transcendental division, and the Two into which the absolute One divides. It is inseparable from an unlearned contemplation and is not understandable without it. As unilateral, it excludes the raging or *absolute* practice, which it would be necessary to call *practicism* in memory of theoreticism. Practicism in the sense of everything-practical is the other effect of terror, the unspiritual identification with being that will have to be civilized precisely through a practice. Non-philosophy seemingly makes use of war and its procedures, not simply against itself but as a reserve where it draws 'weapons' with which it combats war *globally*. This objective is not accessible if they cease to be weapons. We will call 'weapons' those double-headed or double-sided instruments; bifacial weapons that we can turn over in two senses, against others and against the self, it is their most universal definition and that which makes weapons analogous with the World or a microcosm. But they lose their original form and here call for another structure different from the microcosm, a structure of unilaterality, now a unifacial instrument for a work of human struggle that definitely can be the suspension and defeat of the war that is only war. As with all concepts, the concept of war must be dualysed and lose its unitary massivity, which is precisely that of the Total-war and its reversibility. Non-philosophy is, if needed, a unilateral struggle where the adversary holds itself to a single side in spite of it and in which the form of reversibility of ways is suspended. Non-philosophy is not even the continuation of philosophy by *other means*, the ways of alterity, but by the 'means' devoid of their war-form or philosophy. Unilateral struggle where axioms and theorems are turned once each time rather than once and for all against their original philosophical expositions. It does serve a matter that is theoretical-without-theoreticism, whose essence is practical or unilateral, in liberating a Christ-subject. Axioms and theorems, these are our own methods, us men-without-philosophy, so that we can appropriate religion and adapt the divine mysteries to our humanity rather than to our understanding.

The couple of theory and practice does not therefore contain anything truly original. In a philosophical mode the original is not native to – or for philosophy it is belatedly and only intra-philosophical. The oldest couple after terror and its solitude is that of theoreticism and terrorism, infernal couple of specularity, which nourishes the twin sisters of philosophy and war. Theory as doctrine or ideology is weak and dull, giving in ever to compromise, if it is only a completely specular endemic struggle supporting the arousal of the pretenders and their rivalries. As regards war it is well-ordered and coded, scripted it is a 'label' if it is only a systematic, though concealed, barbarism that reappears under the form of the fury of specular destruction of 'civilians'. *The enemy of human kind* is without doubt the knot of theoreticism and terrorism, the ethno-philosophical purification retied to specular purity. They go together into the void of a mirror that reflects itself and does not see itself. The metaphysical battle between Being and Nothingness, those of war, is already a way of refilling this emptiness and expressing it. Philosophy and war are the secular arms of the purism of transcendence.

If auto-specularity is the ultimate core of philosophy, the space of its deployment such that it seems to create itself, it nevertheless misses the mark of the Real after which its most impoverished forms go searching for in the empirical. The auto-specular structure of whole-philosophy is invariant but auto-distorted. It is transcendence fantastically split, at the same time one and two, and devoid of consistency. It can and must be accentuated by the mark and burden of the Real that in the pure core of the philosophical is lacking. Yet, it is the role of religion, from which the philosophical is effectively inseparable, to bring about that affect of the Real. Monotheism in particular benefits from a special privilege of grafting itself to this claim, over-determining it and bringing it that which it lacks. It thus *exentuates* that structure, which is in other respects a creator of indefinitely hollow fantasies, purified of their dross. How does it come to live in this medium?

There are innumerable mixtures of this specular core and religion, but certain monotheisms concentrate that purity and specular rivalry in the crystal of an absolute and repulsive identity, each one from transcendence, and for this reason act immediately directly from the believers that identify with it. The split and distorted unity of philosophy can receive distinct forms but can also be pushed all the way to an identity whose integrity is hyperbolic. The auto-specularity of double transcendence takes the form of a repulsive transcendence, where *the excess is a rearguard action directly exerting itself on believers.* But that absolute monotheism knows at least two distinct fates. The first asserts a God that is 'Alone one', a jealous God who punishes either through his silence or by an excessive absence which opens in the believer's identity an abyss of uncertainty and therefore of responsibilities for the Other, the single identity being responsibility. The second asserts a God that is 'Alone great' who punishes through an excessive presence that imposes on the believer an absolute certainty over its identity, resolving itself to an obedience identical to death. Certain historical differences qualify this structure. Jewish monotheism, implying a negative terror, is peaceful within individuals and effectively becomes dominantly terroristic in the State. Islamic monotheism, implying a positive terror, is instead immediately terroristic in individuals and sects, and dominantly peaceful in the State. The 'clash of civilizations' is also that of religions or rather, in the microcosm of thought, the clash of philosophies.

By its theoretical practice, non-philosophy refuses theoreticism. But by its principle, by the Real that its own, it already refuses specularity and purism in any case. Man-in-person as unlearned knowledge is its final word this side of the One-and-Multiple, of war and peace treaded back and forth in the Great Mirror of transcendence. It is neither One nor Two simultaneously and ignores the sharp edge of absolute positions. The profound reason for this difference is that non-philosophy holds itself in the radical immanence of the Real and philosophy, made worse by religion, holds itself in absolute or repeated transcendence in which it hallucinates the Real. Would there not, however, be a terrorism of immanence that would soothe many philosophies? Immanent or even transcendent, what real difference can one speak of? The difference very much exists, it is that of the *absolute*(philosophical and Gnostic), the always already split mono-absolution, authoritarian and repelling the World, and the *radical* which, by setting man in-Man or the real in-Real, thinks and struggles within the strict limits of this Real without transcendence. By definition, and even if its non-consistency is the object of a misunderstanding, it cannot be a religious fantasy, which can only exercise domination and exploitation, auto-conquest and auto-defence, but can only be the conquest and defence of self as subject *in the Real or in the final Identity near to it.* The meaning of irreducible or unilateral duality protects it from the terrorism of monotheism as the meaning of One-in-person preserves it from philosophical weakening. The subject is in-struggle, an *immanent struggle*, with theoreticism and terrorism, whether it is religious, cultural, philosophical or, why not, simply institutional. The force of the subject is held in the immeasurable weakness of Man-in-person. It does not posses the weapons of theoreticism or terrorism but it knows them and can make use of them *in its own way, neither gentle nor overbearing, but which would like to be rigorous.* Philosophize theoreticism? Terrorize terrorism? Philosophize terrorism? Terrorize philosophy? So many vicious circles and tendencies, so many bad unilateralities, really bilateralities, which mistake the whole of the phenomenon. The heretical struggle is not born from terror or the specular-whole, which it practically undoes, it is born from the being-separate of man that is in-Man.

Why this refusal without a name that rings out as a precaution? Because the most effective destructions are always the most ambiguous. Perhaps they face the Adversary too closely to not be misconstrued by philosophical opinion and, more so, 'intellectual' opinion. Too close, that is to say without habitual mediations, denials and nuances that are those not only of thought in general, but of its philosophical sufficiency or arrogance. It is here then that thought is no longer decisive, as in the idealism and theoreticism of intellectuals, it is decisive only as determined by the Real. Only the Real forces thought into merely being that non-decisional decision (of) self, that is practically, and protects it from its own auto-specular fantasies. It would be necessary to reassemble philosophy and religion, theoreticism and terrorism, under a *Principle of Arrogance* and oppose it to a *justified humility.* In order to make out the face of the Adversary, it is necessary to mix with him and to suffer the extent of his gaze to the point that he believes himself to have grabbed hold of you. Of the two of you, however, only you know that the gaze is nothing, that you are free from the mirror and the speculation and that you are just playing with that haunted gaze which wants to capture yours. The Man-in-person that you are knows without the help of transcendence that it does not leave it by way of a hallucination, that it never entered it there, not by an absolute property or essence but by a knowledge that is not speculative, only as unlearned Man, not as a subject with which it in this regard struggles with. So you will not avoid the great misunderstanding, knowing that the Adversary cannot imagine that you are not on his side and that you do not deny any such adherence. There are impassable misunderstandings, that philosophy cannot overcome (*überwinden*) in its usual way, the operation of non-philosophy is just that of making this visible in philosophy. If there is a criterion for division between theory and theoreticism, rigor and terror, it is unilateral and situated on one side. There is no consensus or common sense, and no longer any dissensus and war, that encompasses the Real or Man-in-person. If dialogue exists, it is for one half.

Non-philosophy is however a practice of Occam's razor. But there are several ways of making a clean cut. There is the theoreticist's way of the Great Philosophical Mirror, pure auto-transcendence without object, and perhaps the frozen mirror of logic, a terror first practised by Wittgenstein in order to impose silence upon philosophers. The terrorist's way, properly so called, severs the intellect itself and strikes down the understanding. Or rather it is the intellect that severs, the understanding that brings about division and death, or so it is faith, the hyper-intellect, that is severed in intelligence itself. One can make a clean slate of the past in the name of the present and become an orphan, that is the Cogito, and above all in the name of an abstract future, that is revolutionary Utopia. In reality the one and the other are full of memories of a past that ceaselessly comes back in these decisions. But against this unitary theoreticism, non-philosophy distinguishes two phases. It makes a clean cut at once with the contents of the past and of the present as well as with their sufficiency, in the name of a radical past and that which does not pass in being-in-the-Past. This is the human immanence of a time-without-consistency, and it makes a clean break from their only sufficiency in the name of the future, thus concrete, which is the subject-in-person.

CALL OF THE FIRST NAMES

The human subject as Future Christ has already responded to the call of God to man through the call of human first names. The call of the first names is the call that gets *to the first name* of Man-in-Man or in-Person.

We call forth the 'World', in this way naming the unity of Earth and Heaven, the terrestrial *and* celestial representational system, the unique sphere of the visible and the invisible when this one is already visible, as in the religions, through another trick of the internal eye.

We call forth the 'Living', in this way naming humans as victims and those murdered in the cause of heresy, thereby revealing the nature of it. Their persecution testifies to an experience of the human that is not natural and that is no longer humanist or philosophical; it is a heretical concept of man as in-Person and applies to all men. The other first names like Humans, Christ-subjects, Heretics, etc., do not designate natural men, susceptible to biological life and death, but *insofar as* they exist as Living and are liable to a being-revealed by persecution and assassination. Heretics are living an invisible life, towards which no gaze can turn no matter what its nature, even a spiritual one.

We call forth 'Christ-subjects', in this way naming human beings in-struggle with the World. These are not doubles of the historico-religious Christ, to whom they do however owe the material of his word [*parole*], but his *immanent clones*, Christs determined in-the-last-identity as Man-in-person.

We call forth 'Heretics', in this way naming human beings, their being-revealed by Living, but so in their existence as subjects that Man-in-person determines under the form of a Future Christ. Heretical more broadly understood is itself said of the Human real, of the Living as if they are no longer included in the World but are Christ-subjects revealed by persecution, this is in general the gospel for the Living.

THE MURDERED AND THE PERSECUTED

How is Man-in-Man revealed as a Living, how is a Living possible, that is to say revealed? Philosophy wonders about the death of natural or worldly man and yearns for an ideal life, but heresy presupposes that Life is a first name for the Real and its subject and presupposes that it is given in a radical or non-biological manner. It repeats on all new grounds the Christian problem of salvation, expounding *on which conditions human beings are universally saved within a salvation that is no longer from the world-religion*. The theory of Future Christ makes of the being-murdered and the being-persecuted a universal but real criteria of the manifestation of Life rather than an absurd condition of historical fact. Opposing an ethics of death to an ethics of life, being anti-Aristotlean or anti-Spinozist, is not what matters. The Living, revealed by persecution, we set them outside-heaven-and-earth, outside-world by decision and by axiom, as testimony to a non-natural Life. With Man-in-person, we have the initial conditions to axiomatize and as a result to theorematize life and death, to extract from their natural and social intuitivity, from that which within religion it subsists in. In human beings there is 'a something' of a radically outside-nature, and the World is a fundamental will that persecutes this heresy. Man-in-person is not an empire within the empire of the World but is that from whom the Real takes precedent above those empires that persecute him and who, turning himself into a victim, confesses to his being-human in spite of them.

By a decision of an axiomatic kind, we therefore place the protestations of rational sufficiency and the belief in philosophical and theological opinion between parentheses. We posit that the ethics of transcendence, as much as those of the immanence of the happy life, belong to the World, that the religions of the Book, just as the others, are religions of the death-World. Ethics and religions exude an infantile hope, a yearning for a silly beatitude and bring to light a hypocritical theodicy. They are the devices-of-the-church, they lull human beings into being inserted into the system of Grand Conformity and to make themselves into subjects-of-the-World. This is not therefore another call from transcendence that necessarily must be opposed, another form of faith, but the immanent call of axioms and the response particular to theorems, the Christ-thought. It is more than a fresh philosophical therapy or an effort, duty or work, of memory. It is *a theory and practice of exorcism* of the religious opinion that lies at the heart of the World. Those Murdered in the cause of heresy are not dormant in memory and buried in history. The murder of human beings reveals, in trying to fill it, the gap within the World that *is*

Man-in-person. It is in this completely positive gap, in this inconsist-ency of Life, that a new decision can be captured under the form of axioms and an explication given under the form of theorems, but still practices, of those that are and those that want, among other things, Christian confessions.

## OF LIFE IN THE LIVED-WITHOUT-LIFE

Philosophy is the hunt for a universal term, but one that is neutral and anonymous – reality, being, time, world, one, other, life, pleasure, the neutral itself and, for theology, 'God' is hardly less anonymous. 'The-life' is one of these overly general concepts, a quasi- transcendental objective for designating a certain subjectivity set in the World. Its smooth character, lacking qualities, the interiority and circularity that it preferably designates and the dissolution of the attributes that it programmes – something of a soft and inconsistent middle ground – dooming it to those functions of subjective substitution in totality or substance. It seems to lock up even the ecstatic dimension that at first it necessarily contains, closing this off from itself and intending to speak immanence. But, as life's conquest, this immanence is *radical and no longer absolute,* assuming three reductions of the unitary and philosophical concept of immanence, supposing that we consider it for a moment as this historical problem by means of this simple introduction.

1.   The first reduction has been carried out by Christianity. With its Gnostic nuances, it has revealed Life in the manner of a new transcendental in philosophy's heaven and maybe elsewhere than that heaven. It has split it, distinguishing an immanent Life as proper to saved man and a life of the species and the biological circle, which is the sum of Greek immanence. Philosophy has never wanted or been able to clearly ratify that duality, it has made of life an amphibological concept *par excellence.* Most of the 'philosophies of life', not all, certain of them being more radical in immanence, offer nothing more than the ontological, either explicitly or at best by a residual presupposition. 'The-life' is then a unitary generality, the source of a facile pathos and

of a philosophical biologism which carries in it future aberrations. But the immanence of Christian life is consonant, however distantly, with that of philosophy. It is an immanence of expectation which, being in-Christ, retains the form of a transcendence and a temporal ecstasy.

2.   Historical gnosis undertakes a second reduction, by excluding the expectation outside of the immanence of knowledge that it presupposes, in order to cast it to the exterior, retaining it however through philosophical influence, final witness to our belonging in Time and in the World. The set of the Gnostic apparatus [*dispositif*], immanence of knowledge included, is projected into the transcendence of the Christian religion and of Greek theoreticism, from which it takes over. It turns to a mythology and anthropological imagination, but it sets in its centre man as knowledge, which we will quickly repeat *untaught or unlearned* (to distinguish it from *docta ignorantia*), and affirms his being-immanence against his being in waiting or in faith.

3.   There is then necessarily a third reduction if one provisionally considers the problem at first under the historico-worldly point of view. It consists in expelling all transcendence to the periphery of Life and in positing that Life is found in itself and even found only *in-Life*, this is why it is without ontological consistency. This is not to nullify the transcendence of the World, it is to ensure it autonomy, although relative rather than absolute. Life ceases to be ecstatically in-waiting for a self and Christ. In the place of 'the-life', in its unitary generality, we substitute, but not in the same place, the 'being-in-Life' that makes man. A *philosophy of radical immanence* that would take Christianity as an object to elucidate what would best make a life most importantly transcendental, and secondarily real. Being-in-Life as being the non-consistent Real is the rock of non-Christianity. But Life is not above all productive or auto-generative and so it is first transcendental. The old problems of beginning and generation are for it not posed and we prefer to designate it by the paradoxical use of the term Living and even, according to our writing, *Lived-without-life*. Life is 'isolated from' . . . , from itself and not reflected in itself. It is more neutral even than Being or pleasure but ontologically and anonymously neutral and so it is radically humane and indivi-dual. Without ability or perfection,

without consistency in general, it can determine, but only in-the-last-identity *as determined and not as determining*, a transcendental Christ-subject which is in-Life for-the-World. 'I (am) in-Life, therefore I am in it for-the-World,' is the new cogito in which the Future Christ performs, that is to say every man or every Lived thing [*Vécu*] that becomes a subject.


MAN-IN-PERSON: CRITIQUE OF THE TRINITY

Christianity, but more so gnosis, indicates to us Man-in-person as final identity for a theory of religious experience. The man of whom we speak is his own real identity, the irreducible core which makes him human and does not just differentiate him from the rest of Creation, to which he otherwise belongs, but from this as well. Understand then that this real and not transcendent identity (in-Man) is the phenomenal content of that which theologians sought as 'person' when composing the Trinity. The person constituent of the theological 'three persons' conveys the prejudices of anthropology and Greek ontology and must not only be deconstructed but, as we have said, 'dualized' or withdrawn following the rules of unilateral duality, which is the way that Man-in-person structures his relations in the World and the practice [*usage*] which he makes of it. We have not called 'person' but 'in-Person' the Identity or the One proper to humans and those subjects to which they transmit them via the operation of cloning, a rigorous formula of the immanent begetting of Sons of Man, in order that the theoretical sense of immanence honours common speech here. In this way non-Christianity develops the non-theological phenomenal content of the Trinity, without making exception for the Holy Spirit, equivalent to the auto-encompassing sufficiency of philosophy, and which it will understand as the Holy Love which mysticism alone gives an image.

If the three persons-in-one of the Trinity traces a closed system like the philosophical triad or the structure of the Philosophical decision (2/3 and 3/2), as Hegel exploited it, and does nothing but testify against the stranglehold of philosophy as a Greek way of thinking, then non-Christianity will oppose to them not a unique person whose identity may be dialectical, or an infinite multiplicity of persons (Nietzsche) who repeat the system, but rather a unique 'essence' of 'in-Person'. More a non-essence than an essence in the final state of auto-position, Man-in-person is a real cause. He is not a prototype since he is not primary but possesses only the primacy of the Real and thus forbids all reconstitution of a Trinitarian system. In-Person signifies that the World is consequently already for him also given-in-Man, rather than created, and already deprived of its folly of self-importance that decreed it uncreated for the Greek or indeed created for the Christian. It is why Man-in-person may *clone* (*give or produce in-One*) from himself a Son, a subject generated-without-birth. A subject crucified in his way by the self-importance of the World and in the same operation by which as cloned it conquers the death-World.

Thus we will differentiate three instances indicated by 'in-Person':

1. Man, Uncreated-in-person *par excellence* as cause of two other 'in-Persons' (and not of their being-in-the-world);
2. the Son of Man as Future Christ, who is the subject, that is to say the World in-Person just as given-in-Man rather than in-World and delivered from the Principle of Sufficient World;
3. the Holy Love as erotic unition of Christ-subjects.

All are non-conceptual symbols, they do not simply oppose themselves to the concepts of onto-theo-logy but rather make a certain use of it ruled by unilateral duality. They undo the supposed universal validity of Christian anthropo-theo-logy and insofar as it conserves Greek ontological presuppositions even Gnostic anthropo-theo-logy. Much as onto-theo-logy has the nature of a system and so leads to dogmatism and conservatism, so non-Christianity is in practice a striving to forge from doctrine a theoretical instrument of salvation for man-in-the-World and for the World itself. For the spirit of the closed system which besieges faith, subjecting man by making him believe in his alienation and sin, non-Christianity substitutes an organon of liberation adequate to the non-consistency which makes it incorruptible as Man and corruptible only as a subject.

## NON-CONSISTENCY OF MAN-IN-PERSON

Let this be the axiom which reformulates the above, *Man-in-person has primacy over essence and existence, human beings do not exist except (as) in-Man.* When Man-in-person appears, the systems of theological, philosophical, and humanist primacy and precessions is knocked down. Man, if he can still refer to himself with this unitary generality, is so inconsistent that he is *par excellence* able to be designated by several first names, symbolized, formalized and deprived of their philosophical sense. As Real he can claim to be a Stranger, an existant-subject-Stranger or Neighbour. Now according to mysticism, he can claim to be like a Future Christ or like the subject that Future-exists [*existe-Futur*]. So many aspects of a style rather than particular systematized styles in 'the-style' of 'the-thought', of positions of thought rather than particular philosophical positions, which are simple material.

Without essence or consistency? Lacking consistency indeed lays claim, in a unitary and philosophical manner, to the multiple or multiples in contrast to the arithemetico-metaphysical One of Unity, but it lays this claim in a radical way from the only Identity that is not just dedicated to difference or division and which remains not immanent (to) self but in-One. Unlike the living others, Man-in-person does not have ontological or religious consistency, he is, as Real, without principle or dogma, without faith or law, but he is consequently the only one living capable of aiding the world in extracting himself from its sufficiency. This Real determines religion and the Christianity-world by removing them from the World. *Man (in-person) is the only being which is not religious as a metaphysical 'animal' endowed with an essence, but which practices only for that reason a religious relationship to the world and makes a World of religion.* Only an atheist practice can make God and Christ intelligible without simply renouncing them or believing in them, an atheist practice without-(doctrinal) atheism, like a radical atheist Man-in-person, but as such without any 'man' of philosophy. Man-in-Man is not strictly speaking a nothing or gap in Being, its failing or fault, or an aleatory point of the World – negative onto-theo-logy – but *the negative condition, which is to say necessary but not sufficient, which determines or clones a subject, a Son of Man, taking leave from the man-world and the God-world.* Without-consistency, only the radical Identity can be this in spite of or because of the paradox that dooms unity, precisely unity and not identity, to consistency.

We human beings are first gnosis, knowledge and not faith, and this 'unlearned knowledge' which is the vision-in-One is *so* absurd that the paradox fades away – this is our dualysis of *credo quia absurdum* [I believe because it is absurd]. We never were of a Worldly nature, even if we have not ceased to participate in it (the true participation is in the World and from there in Ideas). Un-clean and un-wordly [*Im-mondes*], human beings defeat the main adversary, the coalition of God and Logic in transcendence, whose onto-theo-logy is ultimately an idealist and Greek version. Non-consistency is not the nothingness of being or essence, it is that which can determine them because it is not convertible into them. Thus Man-in-person, or even the subject or Son of Man, is not created *ex nihilo* by a *ens supremum* and does not possess the ultimate consistency of the creature. Every being of this kind belongs to the hell of onto-theo-logical imagination, in the fable of creation.

However open it may be, 'the-Christianity' is still a system-religion in convertibility and triad, an aborted and normalized madness that secures in a hallucinatory way its appropriation of Man-in-person. Non-Christianity breaks it down by dualysing the unitary 'essence' of theologico-humanist man and gives him another birth, that of a Future Christ, separated *from* the World and so giving aid to it all the more. As for Gnostic resentment against God, the World, and Creation, which brandishes against them a spiritual fire, one can rather see it as an occasional cause for a non-Christianity that does not respond to the fire of persecution with the fire of intransigence.

## FOR A UNIFIED THEORY OF CHRISTIANITY AND HERESY

The historically dominant Christianity, the one which has given place to a *Principle of Sufficient Church* – from here it will become a question under this name, not of the gnosis which accompanies it – is a *system* of representations and dogmas, of practices and powers [*pouvoirs*]. Like every system, it is traversed by means of a great organizational division out of the edges from which it grows and develops. There is a difference here from philosophical systems that are partitioned according to the dominant (but not unique) axes of truth and appearance (or illusion from the point of view of that has the theory of that partition as an object), for a religion has as its principle or dominant difference that of orthodoxy's division, from the rigour of orthology (as the policing of opinions or dogmas) and heresy, that it sometimes mixes [*se mélange*] with the philosophical that it anyhow cuts again. Christianity overdetermines these two differences by way of God as Christ and World as sin. Thus certain representations have been thrown to the periphery or reputed as 'heretics' by those others who triumphed over it and who call themselves 'orthodox' or 'true' Christianity. This is at least its complete concept, where the heresies are interior and exterior to the core of orthodoxy's constant following its formation, development and affirmation. The line of partition that separates the unique and constantly evolving orthodoxy from multiple heresies has not ceased to move and displace itself according to historical forces created from new distributions and new chicanes.

Heresy is habitually declared 'Christian' by a theology and Church becomes dominant, which judges it nevertheless contrary to their dogmas. This ambiguous theoretical statute is a form of quasi-philosophical mixture, 'the-Christianity' thus assuring the ideal unity of the dominant Church and heresy within which we later call the 'over-church' [*sur-église*]. It suffices that a Church, which is to say the materiality of a certain number of operations intended to produce and secure belief, identifies itself with a different doctrinal variant, and proclaims itself the true and unique religion according to an archaic gesture of *epekeina* common to religion and philosophy, so that it poses the exteriority and the dissidence of other variants, like heresies, and gives itself the right to reduce and subdue them. That is the most general phenomenal content of the *Principle of Sufficient Church*. That structure has its function in the limiting of the reach of heresy by authoritatively deciding on its nature, in rejecting it in exteriority and alterity. It prepares the greatest violence, from which one sees that philosophical forcings are homologous to these without always being as severe.

However, these considerations do not belong to our problem or are nothing more than preliminary to it. How to build up and govern the line of partition of the 'true faith', in some ways a 'bio-theology', is not even our object. Rather, we are able to make another use of heresy, that of an ingredient for a *unified theory* (precisely without theological or philosophical mixture) of Christianity and heresy. This 'non-Christian heresy' will be the *modelling* intended to render intelligible Christianity and its faith, which means: not repeating them in their explication or their 'intelligence'. How to transform the hierarchical unity of orthodoxy and heresy such that they regain equal right within a new thought, putting an end to the violent acts of orthodoxy, without any longer claiming to make of heresy a new principle of absolute rebellion which risks simply reversing the historical state of things and of maintaining the religious exploitation of man under another form? Unlike those who believe in a heretical spontaneism, often every theo-mytho-logical imagination, a certain dogmatic rigidity may be conserved as necessary *under a theoretical form transformed by theorems that remove its pretensions to domination*. As for the shamed [*honnie*] and persecuted rebellion, it may still be saved from its 'revolutionary' violence and naivety. *A non-Christian science is still a science, but unifying the orthodox Christian and the heretic in-the-last-identity by the Man-in-person.* Still it is necessary to find the principle that makes it clear that this cannot simply be a new syncretism or a religion repeating a classical model, a principle that is not drawn from Christianity or from any religion, but also no more from any immediate affirmation of heresies or gnosis. It will be, we have said, the 'vision-in-One' or the 'Man-in-Man'. Future Christianity is the theory of a heretical Christ that unifies in-Man, that is to say in-the-last-identity, outside of the dogmatic authority, of Christic or heretical givens.

Why then 'future'? As for Greek Being and Christian Time, a supplementary mixture in which the philosophy of the preceding century believed itself to have found its renewal, they are dismissed due to their pretensions and handed over to their rightful place, which is the World. These are no more than the modes of symbolization and formalization of the Man-in-person, but they do not determine him. For example 'the-time' allows for a dualysis from its edges in a radical past, the 'in-past' understood as immanence of the Lived, and in a blend which is precisely 'the-time', nevertheless understood as an expanded present in the World beyond simple representation or presence. Their conflict resolves itself as radical or immanent future, dis-enclosed [*désinséré*] in time and which coincides with the subject, the Future Christ. On the basis of the human Real which reduces the sufficiency of religion, and accordingly in addition to the historico-religious arguments, a theorem may be formulated. *In-Man is the radical past which in-the-last-identity determines the Christian and the Gnostic, and every man-of-this-World, as Future Christ.* This is the theorem that demonstrates future life as that of the Christ-man or, again, the Messiah. Because the Lived is without purpose or ecstasy as regards the World, he determines a subject and that subject is for-the-World and Time without being inscribed, even as 'future', in the Time-world.

## THE THREE SOURCES OF FUTURE CHRISTIANITY

Future Christianity finally posses three sources, mixed within 'the-Christianity' in the historical sense, but that we distinguish and isolate in order to determine or unify them in-the-last-identity by Man-in-person, and so differently than in a religion. The first is the properly Gnostic experience of the definition of man by the primacy of knowledge over faith, an untaught or unlearned knowledge that we must radicalize as Man-in-person, Lived-without-life or even as the Real. The second is the more general heretical aspect, of the separation with the World, here extended and universalized beyond its Christian and even Gnostic aspects. The third is the specifically Christian aspect of universal salvation, for the World and for every man, that works through the person of Christ, which we must also radicalize in a Christ-subject. Each of these aspects is dominant in one of these religious experiences but they are present together, measured in different ways, in each of them. Our aim is not to study these measurements and historical combinations but to isolate each time the particular traits of these postures and then, from what then results, to reprocess them in a 'unified theory of Christianity and Gnosis', in a 'non-Christian science' which will no longer obey the law of their historico-religious mixtures, but a completely other 'principal'.

Man-in-Man as being without-consistency, revealed by murder and persecution, is designed to oust the old onto-theo-logy, its diverse branches, and to rethink the Christian and Gnostic experience under ultimately human forms. We do not practice or import any atheism, in undertaking an exercise of thought we sufficiently 'believe' in God, Christ, and more so in the Hell where these shadows live. We believe in a God who claims to take the place of Man-in-person and who is in Hell. In a Hell whose other name is 'the-World' dominated by the Principle of Sufficient Church. But also in a 'non-Christian' Christ rather than an Anti-Christ. This is the human trinity that we oppose to all those all-too-divine religions. A trinity that is no longer of three persons, but of Man-as-final-identity announcing his being-human in the World within the radically subjective figure of a Future Christ that every man who is in-hell has in becoming. In order to construct the concept of non-Christianity and its non-Trinitarian 'in-persons', it is necessary to clarify, under the guard of radical Man and taking leave from their positive historical combinations, the three postures of immanent Gnostic knowledge, of heretical being-separated, and so of the Christian universality of salvation, which we treat as three abstract components. The conception of separated Man is more than the foundation; it the cause which determines the efficacy of this trans-formation of ancient theological personages. We take up each of these sources in order to put together little by little the possible programme of a 'non-Christian science'.

## NOTE

[1] Friedrich Nietzsche (1967), *The Will to Power*, trans. Walter Kaufmann and R. J. Hollingdale (New York: Vintage Books), §685.

# CHAPTER TWO
## Introducing Philosophy to Heresy

THE UNIVERSALITY OF THE HERETIC QUESTION

One of the sources for non-Christianity is the constituent heresy of gnosis, here transformed and radicalized. As a historical occasion it possesses a particular affinity with the Shoah.

One of the assets of the twentieth century is the return of the 'Jewish question' in definitively acute forms. That infinite point of interrogation, having become too heavy, will have made our memory hesitant, a manner of digging into history and opening that which it no longer can close up on itself. Is it perhaps also the unhoped for opportunity to introduce – one does not dare say 'appeal to' [*en appel*] because the only judgment was that 'of God' – a new parallel 'question', that of heretics. If the Shoah is susceptible to the hyperbolic nonsense of a crime exceeding any possible forgiveness that is formed little by little through a thousand troubles and resistances from every origin, then it should be time to wonder if the universal persecution of Gnostics, the planetary reduction of heretics by iron, fire, dogma and insults, if the dead, exterminated because of the claim to an identity which was neither religious nor ethical, are able to receive a meaning and which meaning, already a later and perhaps more impossible meaning than that of those who died because of alterity and 'non identity'.

The comparison of the Shoah with other 'genocides' must not be a levelling, appealing to some historical mean and calculation. The Shoah has repeated in a crucial manner a problem that is without doubt ancient and one that we have hoped to resolve by the means of civil society and philosophy. It does not matter to what extent it is a real or seemingly particular event, it is in any case a *symptom* which can always be analysed and dismembered within relative historical parameters, *can it, without injustice, lay claim to a universal meaning and to having validity for all of humanity*? But posing the question in this way is perhaps too spontaneous and thoughtless. Does it have a single possible universal and what is the status of the particular in relation to it? Is philosophy the unique and definitive master of these categories? Does it not have a power higher than the philosophical universal, for example Alterity and above all Identity precisely as universal determinant? The Jewish feeling of misfortune would assume then a more nuanced evaluation. The historical particular does not have the same sense, universal or not, for the Jews as for the philosophers, who do not speak about the same thing and so needlessly quarrel. From this point of view the Jewish demand has nothing excessive about it, it is not evaluable from elsewhere than from itself, it is the only judge of itself, but there is no need to say that it is without logic or 'irrational'. It is a primary way of limiting the pretention of universality to a *particular universality*. Because the problem concerns the plurality of universals and *a capacity* [puissance] *of thought that would admit their plurality, at the conflicting origin, without relativizing them by a relationship of one to the other, but rather extracting them from their warfare.* And yet heresy, more so than Judaism, can be the opportunity to pose this problem, the chance of freeing the universals from their competition. *The power* [puissance] *higher than the system of the universal and the particular to which it belongs is that of Identity and of the universal to which it belongs.* In the perpetual war in which particular philosophies engage, among themselves and with Judaism, in order to know which is the most universal for man, we substitute the presupposition of Identity and the universality to which it belongs. Of course this Identity is not a unity or of an ontological nature.

Regarding heresy and the crime to which it has been constantly subjected, it is significant that the time of repentance has not yet come. Perhaps it is impossible and it will never come for this crime of which the singular type – the identity – exceeds the juridical generality of a 'crime against humanity' or, more exactly, in revealing the generality's cause. Do we know that the philosophers and theologians never asked for forgiveness? Are they satisfied with 'criticism' and 'reflection', be it of their own tribunal, that of Logos or that of the Church? Even the time of reflection on the humanicide of the heretics is always pre-programmed, as if the problem had been regulated by the crime itself. How else does one imagine a pardon for what man is not able to forgive since he was *the unique object of it as such*? Yet, we will ask, for lack of anything better, that the philosophers, theologians and historians reconsider the 'heretic question' and examine to what extent it is instead heresy which questions their traditional posture and their good conscience, their authority and their prejudices which support heresy.

And since it is memory that still acts as thinking for cultivated humanity and for the intellectuals that represent it, let us recall, then, before proceeding otherwise, that the sentiment of the crimes against heretics has remained vivid among some and survives as a light which is never put out, precisely as a remembrance not submitting to the fluctuations of memory. Heresy was only a question to be resolved as soon as it was asked, and in a sense before even being asked, by violence of the most material and spiritual kinds at the same time. Has the situation changed much between the crime and our memory of the crime? That memory is not fundamentally different from that of the criminal who retains the reality of his crime [*forfait*] in the ether of ideality and the fluctuations of meaning. Have we done something other than add bad conscience to the archive of crime, other than stretch, dilute and idealize this? Here it is no longer about wanting the past in order to cultivate it or transform it; not even of keeping alive the memory which makes us hostage to history. Precisely there is a past so radical, we will say so *outside-memory*, the crime has affected man so profoundly that he has become *an evident unconscious or better still an unlearned knowledge* of modern man and which he defines perhaps more profoundly than the exercise of memory. If the Jewish affect is that of being-hostage, the affect of the heretic is that of being-victim. Not in annoyance at the philosopher and their hatred of the victim, the heretics have been those men from whom we learn precisely that memory is not the essence of man or the final justification of history, that it is instead the faculty of the Grand Reconciliation and of Regained Conformism. They impel us to invent another solution than that of anamnesis on which the old consumers of the history of philosophy are drunk.

## HERETICAL REVELATION

The heretics reveal to us that man is in an ultimate way that being, the only one, who endures crime and is characterized by the possibility of being murdered rather than simply persecuted and taken hostage, exterminated as 'man' rather than as 'Jew'. Why ultimate? *Because man is without-consistency, he is on principle, in contrast to other beings, able to be murdered, he is even the Murdered as first term for heretical thought and for the struggle that it performs.* Of course in this theorem there is not any justification for crimes against humanity, on the contrary, rather the necessity of distinguishing the Murdered from the murderer, of breaking their vicious circle and of taking the victim as the last point of view on history against its denigrating philosophers. This is what we call *the hypothesis of murdered men*, which we turn into a theorem according to man, annihilated in the fire of the stakes that were not completely spiritual.

Because the heretics have been 'a problem' for the dominant Churches, their extermination has not been one . . . But suppose for an instant that they were not 'put in question' because they refused in their most intimate being precisely to be 'in question' and the object of a question that is by definition interminable. For the heretics, being put-in-question by an authority that presupposed them to be openly questionable is a miserable vicious circle and it is the circle of crime or violence. On that hypothesis, could they not be made to show the crime, to which they have been subjected, as an exemplary crime which unveils the essence of crimes against humanity and pulls apart its unitary generality? As a true problem, philosophically and theologically insoluble and even unable to be formulated, but soluble under the conditions of man as the ultimate Real? Perhaps we must begin by changing the posture of thought and taking on other initial terms, speaking of a problem rather than of a question, and a soluble problem for the human victim as being 'outside-of-question'. The ready made formula of the 'heretic question' is a completely unhappy and ill-adapted sum, already philosophically 'well-ordered'. These new conditions, theoretical and human in the same movement, give us the hope of being able to *universalize*, without *revising*, the question of the Shoah.

A call to think heresy and its extermination always risks repeating the bad habits of Christian theology, leading at best to a 'revision', a retraction or a new appropriation of the wholly hermeneutic type, that of the bad conscience. But the project of re-activating human reality, gnosis, is completely different from its meaning for a religious conscience. In gnosis it goes from man and no longer from the World, from the One-in-person and no longer from Being or the Other. The human Real revealed by heresy in an original way and the heretical practice of thought which it reveals, excludes the authority of the ontological and philosophical apparatus but not at all the dominant use of its materiality.

We have said that they equally require the Christian experience of life-in-Christ, which has contributed a certain share to the constitution of gnosis. From that angle, our project takes the form of a tentative non-Christian heresy, in the sense that non-philosophy usually understands that 'non-' as a universalization by Identity rather than as negation by Being. It is the outline of a 'unified problematic' that is not destined to guide the theological and historical science in their relationship to gnosis, but to treat them in their positivity as the material of a heretical non-Christian practice. From that thought the cause, the procedures and the rules are those which determine Man-in-Man. They are neither theo-logics in general nor are they philosophical and historical. It goes without saying that the various real gnoses [*gnoses*] are nothing more than material, fundamental like Christianity, but with which it is a question of producing a non-religious and simply human thought. So, you will not find here any exegesis of historical gnosis and its prejudices, which are those of a heavily transcendent imagination, something mythological, but rather an attempt at unloosing the original nucleus, as it were its specific difference in relation to a sufficient Christianity and philosophy.


HERESY AS RADICAL IDENTITY

'Heresy', a concept that is as unstable and elusive as its object, transparent and secret as heresy itself . . . In its religious and theological usage, it is purely negative and serves to denounce, condemn and deny what it seemingly describes, *performatively or by the same act of its description*. A description that is immediately a denunciation of its object is the primary significance of this concept. We make it the symptom of immediate and quasi-performative identity (opposites) and we make use of it like a first name in a scientific discipline of religions.

If this concept exists overwhelmingly in the religious and theological field, it seems unthinkable in the philosophical and metaphysical field where it does not manifest except at a distance. The metaphysical forgetting of heresy is its second aspect of significance. *What is there in the essence of heresy such that it still has not penetrated philosophy, never acquired the status of a true concept, even a negative or polemical one?* What is there in heresy, having only an essence, so that this theme is immediately present or immediately absent in two related fields?

We will neither engage in an interpretation or hermeneutic, nor in a deconstruction of heresy. We transfer under these precise conditions that historico-theological concept into the sphere of thought. We conserve, trying to elucidate it and render it positive as being the same heresy, that ability to identify so radically the contraries that we no longer know if it affirms or condemns absolute evil or absolute good. It seems in any case to forbid logically sensible discourse. Can an absolute evil only be described and understood *even after explanations* as the heresy hunters said? Is the heretic the *absolutely singular or rather really the radically identical?* An object of a radical forgetting without remainder, this identity performed right through is inaccessible as well in simple repression, immediately present and 'evident' for the Churches but as the same evil. Such a manner of manifesting itself is without doubt original and does not fall outside the philosophical laws of presence and absence, of repression and anamnesis. This paradox of heresy, we make it its 'essence' but an essence of 'without-essence' and we wonder what the relationship is between this Without-essence and the essence by which, inevitably, we designated it.

Heresy comes under the most unsuspected radical 'logic' and its philosophical paradoxes. We try to update it, leaning on its pre-suppositions and the wave of its contrasting usage in order to clear it of its enigmatic depth and its performative character. Under what conditions, of a quasi-philosophical and no longer positive-religious nature, can we unleash the nucleus of this 'logic'? Heresy becomes a category for philosophy if, for its part, philosophy changes systematically and passes from metaphysical and theological Unities, respectively from the form-Being and the form-Church, to non-ontological and non-theological Identities. The reciprocal pollination of a thought of the One and a heretical position is not new in history (Gnostic dualisms), but it becomes so when the One is finally thought in its own essence, which is from being the Without-essence and distinguished from its Greek, Jewish and Gnostic usages. It traces, then, a new programme for thought. It is not only about making a use of an adjective, applying it to those notions that it ordinarily does not support (an essence, a multiplicity, a practice, a heretical use of philosophy), but about the most decent human contents, that which humans are: in-Decent.

## GNOSIS AGAINST PHILOSOPHY

Gnosis is more human but not more 'existential' than philosophy and that dominant form of Christian faith. It asserts with unequalled depth the questions which bring forth Man and the World rather than Being and thought, but above all asserts them with a method that is human or said 'of-the-last-identity', overturning the philosophy that it makes use of because its questions assume in reality the essential response already given – there is no salvation in the World or history, salvation is already *given* although still without efficacy and expressed in a special struggle that shows its primacy.

Gnosis introduces a new question in relation to the question of Being – What is the *Eon*?[1] What is the *in* (one) and the *they* or *one*(being) in their unity, without doubt, but in the unity as One rather than as Being? The One and Being arrive in thought as a coupling, which signifies that historical gnosis did not break with any philosophy. It is nevertheless a question that is no longer 'fundamental' and no longer wants to be, in so far as it refuses the anonymity of Being as horizon aiding a psychological, spiritual, and living '(being-) one', in the indelible feature of humanity and identity.

While man is interpreted from anthropo-logical presuppositions and gnosis, from its position, understood as mythology, there is no chance of seizing the anti-ontological originality of the question of *l'e(-on)*, of the in(-one), its innovative strength equal to that of the Jewish affect of the Other, the hatred in which philosophy welcomes and envelops it.[2] Without doubt Heidegger has signalled that the *in* was given with the *one*, but that was in order to better couple Being and the One and affirmed the final authority of Being over the One. This was giving in to Greek thought, to the worldly anonymity, crushing once again the Gnostic rebellion of Life and evidently misunderstanding that Christianity had also, in a more hesitant way, displaced the subject's centre of gravity from the Cosmos towards human Life.

Gnosis shatters the aporetic relations of ontology, anthropology and humanism and not only those of God and man. Facing unitary desire, more-than-gregarious, of the churches, gnosis has put to work its multiplicity, and against their unitary division its spirit of *separation*. But these are now the symptoms for us in terms of the heretical research of Identity and the spirit of the Multitudes. As heresy, gnosis claims to be in identity and multiplicity, in solitude as much as in the multitude. It is any onto-theo-logy whatsoever that must be modified according to that decisive irruption of man in the Greek onto-cosmo-logy. Modern philosophy will try the most to benefit. But man and God are not identical in a Unity or a Same (in dialectical closeness). It is however the thesis of much of philosophy, or even the 'grand' philosophy, theologico-idealist which, from that point of view, seems to appropriate gnosis. But that is just the least inventive side of gnosis, the most transcendent and specular, the side of the God-man and of their amphibological combination. Philosophy is all the more allowed to gain by a Gnostic 'deviation', internal and external, since these 'deviations' have always mixed with Greek philosophy. Gnosis described in a manner that is still religious and transcendent, philosophically 'unilateral' and abstracting the World, in a style reduced to a division to which Unity cannot be opposed. But it is not Unity or the infinity that can be 'opposed' to it without giving place to its opposition, of the spiritual and the infinite; it is the Identity-in-person.

Gnosis, above all Mandaean Gnosis, along with Christianity, is one of the greatest thinking about Life, and it wants to radically distinguish itself from the thought of Being without always reaching precisely there for the reasons of philosophy. Maybe the Gnostic withdrawal of Life, which returns ontology to mythology and to the imagination, is the chance or the condition that we will call 'transcendental' in order to *model* (this is one of our objectives) Christianity and remove it from the authority of the churches and the explication of theology. But consequently here it is hardly used for anything, except to philosophize, wanting to break in a sufficient-heretical way with Christianity. On the other hand it becomes possible, postulating the identity of the first names of the One, from the Living-without-life and of the Man-in-person, to construct a model of God himself, the God of onto-theo-logy evidently, so the one of faith-as-expectation-of-Life. And a *modelling* of God certainly becomes more pertinent to its object than that imaginary model of the Great Watchmaker.


SAVING GNOSIS


The divine creation – the World – is a failure, this knowledge is one thing that gnosis acquired. As an argument, it comes to support the most theoretical reasons that campaign for the abandonment of the metaphysical thesis of creation. But what is it that nevertheless has failed in gnosis and so simply opposes it to constituted Christianity, which it cannot then uproot? All its theoretical, theological, and psychological apparatuses are deployed in the most extreme transcendence. It wants an exteriority *absolutely of the World, thus still in the World* to which it remains nearby, without, for example, achieving or losing, because of Christianity and philosophy, the sharp edge and strength of Judaism. As for the remainder, gnosis must be saved, and not by itself.

The fundamental distinction between gnosis and non-Christianity (the most unapparent also) is that of the transcendent and religious reality of man (in the World) and of the real-and-transcendental phenomenality of Man-in-person. Only the transcendental philosophers like Kant and Husserl are able to give an idea of this kind of distinction. Religious gnosis is realist and metaphysical, worldly and 'cynical'. Non-Christianity is transcendental, moreover in a sense that is no longer philosophico-worldly as in these writers. It is a function, but in-the-last-identity, of the philosophico-worldly transcendental, that is to say idealist. It is no longer logical ideality that saves the transcendental character of thought, it is its cause as 'Real-of-the-last-identity'. How to free the heretical affect from its premium mixture with the ontological horizon? Is it about reprocessing that ambiguous material according to an exposition that is at once (close to the in-the-last-identity) a true axiom (rather than a postulate that is ontological and so intuitive, as are those of the religious gnosis) and a true transcendental theorem (that relates to that material-mixture which is the Gnostic onto-mytho-logy)? That declaration therefore subdues the gnosis itself in Man-in-person and says that this is determined-in-the-last-identity.

In passing to the radical identity, non-Christian heresy seems sometimes to turn gnosis inside out like a glove. But the immanence of the in-Man is not the symmetrical invagination of a bulging relief, the concave of a convex, the verso of a recto, it abandons all religious topology of salvation. It also seems to engage in the multiplication of entities, the splitting of intermediaries, for example where it speaks of the cloning of a subject as we do here. But the in-Man is rather the radical Simple that simplifies the World and philosophy as a technology of alloying thought and the rule of the intermediaries. Even the clone of the Son of Man does not specularly split the man-world but gives it its transcendental identity. The Future Christ explains and determines the Christ-world precisely in eliminating from oneself every specular relationship to the World.

The necessity for salvation is universal. If the Christ assumed to save and the God assumed to create must be saved in their turn, they can only be so saved by a knowledge, radical in-the-last-identity, in which Christian and Gnostic theology, as well as their mixtures, will be affected by a *non*-universalizing and unilateralizing that will subject them to Man-in-person. *Christ and God determined-in-the-final-identity by the Real rather than realized in and by philosophy (Boehme, Hegel, etc.).* Redemption is a unitary concept, at the same time too simple and subject to uncontrolled division and amphibologies. We distinguish doubtlessly three series of notions, salvation, the saviour, and the saved saviour from the theological side; the in-Man-as-Irredeemed [*Irrédimé*], God and the World, finally the subject-saviour or non-Christian Messiah who justifies them in the measure where they are able to be such from the side of the Real. However, these are not the divisions of a Gnostic theology so wrongly making fun of the amphibologies of Christian theology and philosophy. Salvation is an operation of birth and emergence rather than of restoration or re-creation. That which clones the in-Man forms, if we want it to, a pleroma of non-Christians and, as we said elsewhere, a transcendental city of Strangers, but this pleroma does not double the World, it brings it the identity that it does not have.

## THE BAD THEORETICIAN

'Know thyself' is the supreme temptation proposed to man, as it is to philosophy. The Gnostic does not know, it is not knowledge (of) self but unlearned knowing deprived of all ecstasy. The only knowledge to acquire is that of the World, including what remains there of man. 'Know thyself as you are *in* the World and *for* the World.' If it is necessary to start again completely differently from that failed knowledge that is philosophy, we do not simply reject it on religious grounds like the ancient gnosis rejected the World as evil and illusion. It is our only material, and the science that the Moderns have acquired meanwhile gives us a means of knowing, that is to say of modelling, that complex object, failed knowledge, and a means of making use of it on the basis of Man-in-person which is not modern or ancient. We are the new Gnostics who think that there is a salvation even for evil. Philosophy, form of the World, is our prison but the prison has the form of a hallucination and a transcendental illusion, not the form of flesh – it is itself knowable.

As there is a *bad demiurge*, there is a *bad theoretician*, the Philosopher or the Theologian, who have created a failed knowledge such that we must begin again completely differently, by avoiding the infernal circles to which they have doomed themselves. To the specular theoricism of the Greeks which crosses through everything that is called 'philosophy' and that is so ignorant of the self that it wants to know itself, we oppose rigorous gnosis, a transcendental axiomatic, which begins by the immanent and non-specular knowledge, which does not have the form of a circle, even one squashed onto itself, and which determines theory in eliminating theoricism. This knowledge is on the order of an unlearned experience of unknowing, but it determines a teachable knowledge. Is it a 'twinkle' rather than a flash? A 'particle' of light rather than lightning? We will take these images not as *metaphors* – why not also *epekina-phors*? – but as the attempts of first terms or first images for a visual and imaginal [*imaginale*] axiomatic, that we may accept on its ultimately human beneficial use.


## THE HERETICAL OR SEPARATED REAL

Given without the support of a givenness [*donation*], untaught knowledge, the vision-in-One is not divided like perception between actuality and potentiality, vision and not vision, awakening and sleepiness. The One is the Awakening-in-One. 'Wake up!' is the slogan of the transcendental philosophers (Kant and his dogmatic slumber), of apocalyptics at best and sectarians at worst, but 'I (am) one Awakened, therefore I awake' is the impossible Christianly theorem, even after explications, of the heretics who awaken mysticism itself. The first is the cry of faith and the ultimate injunction of philosophy, the second is the first non-religious gnosis.

Two philosophically contradictory theses form the paradox of unlearned knowing:

1. The One-in-One in the radical sense does not manifest itself in metaphysics, is not intrigued by the conscience or the present and its 'retreat' or its 'forgetting' is radical (in contrast to that of Being).
2. It never lets itself forget, the given-without-givenness excludes forgetting.

The forgetting of the One by the philosophy-world is in-the-last-identity the radical impossibility of forgetting it. Heresy is on the one hand a definitively lost model of thought (there is not a 'question of heresy', while there is a 'Jewish question'), a hopeless thought and so the 'holocaust' has been consummated for a long time, perhaps always. It is a Western outside-memory, a loss without possible return, an immemorial paradigm. On the other hand it is not so lost because it is the essence of thought's non-consistency. By its principle, not to say its historical realizations, heresy is more than a new 'category' of thought, it is its transcendental force. It is not the repressed or destroyed Other of the West; the Jew is. There is a difference of nature between Being and the Jewish experience of Alterity, equally a difference a difference of nature between the Jew and the heretic, between Alterity and the Immanent-in-person.

In order to explain this paradox, we construct the concept of heresy by approximation, as a description which proceeds by simulating the operation of philosophy. Heresy, then, presents several aspects.

1. An aspect of decision, but one which does not take the ordinary ways of the scission or of the division and of their repetition, those of transcendence as split unity or separated from itself, as a divided Absolute. It is performed according to other ways, those of Identity or Radicality, and of the unilateral duality.

2. That decision only has the appearance of a reciprocity, but is in reality a separation, a taking leave, rupture that 'breaks with' the transcendence but that defines itself by a being-separated rather than by an operation of separation since the transcendence already concentrates every thought and its operation. There is a Separated that is never made the object of an operation, it is a decision that is non-decisional (of) self.

3. That decision presents a single side, it is unilateral in relation to the always reversible or bifacial transcendence. It refuses the shares that are the privilege of the World and every technology of philosophical distinctions that take them up again and amplifies them under the form of 'transcendence'. Identity of the *hairesis* rather than bilaterality or duality of the *di-hairesis*, of the dieresis.[3]

4. It is a Separated but can only be autonomous if it is not absolute which is to say relative and bilateral as well – that would be a contradiction in terms –, but radical or immanent, a Separated-by-immanence. This Separated is an Identity, but that is neither the Void nor the Whole, the Separated is 'given-in-a-Separated' rather than given-in-separation.

5. It is a 'presupposed real', an Identity-in-person that determines a thought for the World.
6. These first names, symbols rather than concepts, contribute to the designation of the Real as heretical and designate it as the real desire of philosophy.


## THE ADVENTURES OF SEPARATION

It is impossible to return a human meaning to heresy without a new practice of theory according to the One. It will have to make sure to distinguish the One-in-person from Being and from its contemporary avatars (Difference for example, whether that of Nitezsche-Deleuze, that of Heidegger, or that of Derrida). Heresy does not begin empirically with the refusal of the World or of History as we vaguely say, but *really* with indifference towards the World and *transcendentally* with its refusal or rather its unilateralization. That decision is no longer a sectarian break, or even to say a difference, it is strictly unilateral and derives only from the One-in-person. We will define heresy by the unilateral choice, that which possesses a real-separated cause whose flaw renders it illusory and contradictory (Hegel's objection to unilaterality wrongly understood as abstraction).

From the One as Real, from the vision-in-One, we will say that it is not identical to itself as the Same or as identity as a Principle, but only that it is 'in-One', separated (without operation) from Being, from the Other and from the World, that the heretical Identity is such by immanence and not by opposition or relation to something else. The in-One is no longer the Other-One of philosophy. The paradox that undoes philosophical common sense is that the One-in-One is not a doubling of itself (One-from-the-One), nor a separation of self or division, it is *separated from the World in a immanent manner*. In other words, the One is intrinsically from the order of choice or of the decision, but unilateral and by immanence rather than by an external decision. The One which determines heretical thought is philosophically undecidable and interminable without being the type of undecidable that belongs to the philosophical decision, since it is undecidable by the philosophically undecidable itself.

Several heresies become incarnate in deadly sects but the strictly human Living-without-life demands that we free from the positive and historical forms of heresies an inseparable position of the Untaught and consequently separated (from the) World for all that the radical Living is unseparated [*inséparé*] (from) itself. The historical separation of heresies or the like is the symptom of a being-separated-without-separation, as we have come to see it, or even (though this is the same thing), it is its falsification by the Churches which reject being-separated as *splitting with* them, a misleading interpretation that is naturally followed by the anti-heretic crime. Radical heresy is certainly not a separation-without-separation, a childish contradiction that the dialectic and theology gloriously resolve. Nor is it a 'negative heresiology' made to return reluctantly to the Church. It is a *being-separated* without which there would have been a sectarian operation. While being-separated is represented or imagined as a philosophical division of identity, a partialization, as a fold of separation and the separated, heresy is undone or judged by the transcendence of the churches. More than an error it is a hallucination of the World and theology united. *Immanence separates, transcendence encompasses, but the theo-philosophical mixtures reverse these effects, immanence encompasses, transcendence separates.* It is the peculiarity of the philosophies that they make claims 'from immanence' to operate without saying a word about transcendence, work with it without thematizing it, or not thematizing it except as effect. Restored within the limits of being-separated, heresy must be understood as uni-laterality, not being thus eased or transformed from transcendence but from that which precisely is separated from it. *Being-separated is not a form of onto-theo-logical transcendence and must not be confused with it.* In philosophical terms, it is real and therefore possibly transcendental, while transcendence is at best first transcendental and *assumed* real whatever the distinctions that modify it.

As for the 'decisions' of language and thought by which we formulate and define heresy, we know that they must themselves be heretical and not philosophical and theological orthodoxies.

Though they are pronounced from a philosophical origin, they are treated in two stages:

1. They are separated-without-separation from the unitary philosophical pretention that was initially theirs concerning the Real, from the pretention of the Church and from the sufficiency of Dogma on their being-human.

2. They must be furthermore dualysed (object of a separation, this time, but as effect of the unilateral duality of the Real and the World) in their content and their philosophical meanings, their functioning and their conceptual operation. This is why the pronouncements of future Christianity, all being pulled from philosophy and theology, continually pass from the state of dogma or of 'revealed truths' to the state of material for axioms (as they have lost in-the-last-identity their truth and their pretention concerning the Real) and of theorems (as their structure is transformed according to the 'syntax' of unilateral duality).

It is thus the non-consistency of human Living that says that it is separated from the consistency of an essence or from Being, this is what the heretics have revealed to us and it challenges philosophy and theology. If they at least had accepted making being-separated a new principle, a heresiarchy [*heresiarchie*] with its heresiarchs, a compromise would have been possible, a peace treaty and a sharing of influences. But they want nothing to do with hearing the objurgations and the reprimands of the churches, they speak to the ignorant people, to the untaught multitudes and in the most theoretical language, the most replete of 'principles' and concepts. We have never known if they believed in these principles or if they mocked them. Only the fire of the stake, obviously . . .

## HERETICAL DECISION AND PHILOSOPHICAL DECISION

The *hairesis* is, in the first philosophical and theological appearance, the choice of unilaterality, party, faction or sect. It is opposed to the dual separation that is in the end reversible and totalizing of the philosophical decision. It is the reputed impossible choice, faulty and transgressive, from that which should not have been selected, from the dissident minority rather than from authority, from the part rather than the whole, from heterodoxy rather than from dogma. The Whole does not form the object of a choice, but at best of a decision that again places the decision maker in the circuit, combining the decision and the undecidable. It is the unilaterality of heresy, its abstract character, which forms its philosophical difficulties and, even more so, its theological ones. But who does not see that this conception of heresy is inevitably that which forms a system with dogma and authority, which is posed *a priori* by either philosophy or the sufficient Church, which are consequently legitimate victors? The contempt the victorious have for the intelligence of heretics and minorities is unfathomable in its naiveté. It would have to give heresy the real basis for an immanent being-separate or without a process of separation or, failing that, all the ground which it refuses, in order to get out of its philosophical aporias and create an operational instrument.

Since its commencement through to its maturity the great principle of philosophy is the division and the unity of the Absolute, the identity of difference and identity, a schema which supports infinite variations of which Hegelianism is the most accomplished. In heresy, borrowing from that vocabulary for a moment, the decision and the undecidable, difference and identity, distribute themselves otherwise than they do in philosophy. The division is without unity but not without identity, difference and identity are identical but precisely as 'in-the-last-identity', without forming a synthesis or a system, without a new, superior identity, re-identification or re-affirmation. This terminology risks inducing unnoticed philosophical prejudices, in particular identity understood as 'unity' and division understood as 'difference'. All these confusions are concentrated in the philosophical and religious *Absolute*, the great adversary of heretical radicality. Whose interest is it to confuse the absolute and the radical, to make the latter a catchall synonym for the former or not to care at all? Curiously one may have confused identity with singularity, unilateral choice with bilateral decision, and heresy with partisanship and the sectarian spirit, as if identity was devoid of universality and reconcilable only with singularity. But there is a universality higher than the concurrence of contraries, than the synthesis or the system, and a style more radical than that of singularity. Heresy is grace given and tuned [*accordée*] to the requirements of a thankless philosophy that finally ceases to wallow in its bad conscience and ceases too to debate in a perpetual crisis.

How does one become a philosopher, for what reason or absence of reason? Philosophy has examined this question without reaching a stable conclusion, which it excludes by nature. But how does one *become* a heretic? Surely at this time this question is inadequate. One is tempted to pose the problem under the form of an alternative: whether to go past and continue otherwise or clone and determine in-the-last-identity? Either analysing and synthesizing or dualysing? That seems to be the new crossroads for thought. But that alternative is still from a philosophical logic. The heretical choice may not be the choice 'of . . .' heresy, in the sense where heresy has already determined it. It is a unilateral image of the Identity-in-person, no more a choice between one of the terms to the exclusion of the other; that of the part, the faction, the sect, and no longer of becoming, passage, or transition. Its identity, its non-participation in Being or in the Other, in ontology or in Judaism, testifies to its being-performed. The 'hairetical' [*hairétique*] choice is immanent and without reason, without essence or an always transcendent foundation.[4] But that it does not obey the Principle of Reason and that of philosophical sufficiency renders it as much as is necessary, as the Real itself.

Heresy is the only choice that is as such radically autonomous in comparison to its motifs and motives but which is able to-determine-them-in-the-last-identity and which, *to this extent, occasionally* depend on it. It is the logically and philosophically impossible choice, but real as immanent. That which the Principle of Reason refused heresy under the names of difference, of scission, of break, of decision, and not just of totality, the Man-in-person gives to it and gives himself as *a choice which, far from being subjected to them, determines itself in the ultimate manner, therefore without creating them, its conditions of impossibility and possibility.* The heretical imperative, if there is one, is not a performation *to be attained and somewhat heteronomous*, but a thinking according to a Performed which brings about a 'final-identity'.[5] The philosophy that pronounced the *cogito* is close to heresy, but only as its own orphan, not as a radical clone of philosophy. An axiom and/or a theorem of heresy is that the part determines in-the-last-identity the Whole, but only has validity if it is radically immanent as part and thus assured of not becoming again a whole. One suspects that heresy effectively shatters the logic and phenomenology of wholes and parts, but only the Radical identity moves it from the state of an overtaken philosophical aporia interiorized in the state of the performed decision. Man as Performed-without-performation determines every decision as non-decisional (of) self.


## HERESY AND DIFFERENCE

Our conjuncture is that of a return to the problem of decision in philosophy (Fichte/Heidegger/Derrida) and ethics. All metaphysics from Heraclitus until Nietzsche gathered around the concept of 'Difference', to which Heidegger opposed his own interpretation of difference as a 'step back' [pas arrière], but it remains, under these two distinct modes, the ultimate Greco-Western invariant. And yet difference, too, contains a unilateral decision. It is a break that is united, a disjunction that is also inclusive or unitive, a tear that gathers up, etc. Even understood from the infinite variations in the proportions and economy of disagreements [différends] or of the differe(a)nce given its variety in philosophy generally and specifically in that of the twentieth century. Unilateral in its manner, each time it is the impossible choice, suppressed or suspended, from one side against the other and the affirmation of its autonomy. But it interiorizes the unilaterality and suppresses the autonomy from the chosen side, because it is also in the long term more or less the unity of two sides, their reversibility, or even their reciprocity of background [arrière-plan]. Even when it deconstructs itself, philosophy remains an ulterior motive [arrière-pensée]. In its Hegelian, Nietzschean, Heideggerian, Derridean, etc., modes, difference respects these invariant features which content themselves with twisting and complicating the Greek metaphysical paradigm. Thus the metaphysical emergence of the decision 'in favor' of Being or of its deconstruction, the irreducibility of the philosophical act to the sciences, techniques, and theology, point paradoxically towards the undecidable grounds of every decision. The sociological and systematic theories of the decision,

FUTURE CHRIST

following metaphysics, can only show the impossibility or the circularity in a technologically intense environment. But the metaphysical and theological 'decision makers' are only particular and self-important representatives and we must oppose them to heretics.

We may expect from a non-philosophy of heresy a renewal of decision theories. The problem is finding the condition that renders the choice *radically autonomous* in relation to its purpose, motives and conditions. In general the decision is empirically or ontologically enclosed, including as the activity of a will, in the taking of an economic decision or a rational calculation. Against the conceptions that make a mixture woven into the Undecidable, it is necessary to return the decision to its strength, unilaterality and autonomy in relation to its 'reasons'. To give it a necessary cause, but not a restrictive one because it is without sufficiency in relation to reality, a unilateral or separated cause in order to get itself away from every empirical decision or choice 'between'. The One-in-One is this Undecided-in-person which neither breaks into the decision nor dissolves it, which no longer decides itself by an ultimate causality of self and by simple 'opposition' to the sphere of empirical decisions. Heresy is the decision, not in favour of singularity, but *according to* Identity, unilateral since it decides 'in favour of', if one can still say it, that which does not allow for an account of its decision and is foreclosed to it.

The heretical choice is rigorously unilateral only if it is directed towards the One and ceases to repeat difference. In reality the One is so much in-One that it is not an object of choice. One does not choose the Real as one chooses a being or even Being, one does not decide in favour of the One against something else because it is opposed to nothing. The Undecidable is the cause rather than the object of the 'heretical' decision. It is no longer the undecidable and universal grounds in every decision, it is the immanent Undecided and thus heteronomous to the decision. It is not undecidable in the sense that Totalities, Unities, Universals (Churches, States, World, History) claim to be in order to conserve their power over individuals and reject heresies or denounce them as 'unilaterals'. The Real is no longer the Undecidable as passivity without counterpart or with a compliment of activity. The hyperbolic passivity in front of the Other and the passive heretic, divine election and the choice undecided-in-the-last-identity must be distinguished, as the *assumed real* break (as alterity), thus first

50

because real (it goes from critique to deconstruction), and unilaterality, which is not only first but determined in-the-final-identity by the Real that it is not. The priority of beginning is always determined by the Real, either immediately, that is philosophy, or in-the-final-identity, that is heresy.

We understand then that the major objective of unilaterality can be interpreted in two opposing senses (a) from the point of view the totalities of heretic-religious, from which the sectarian or the dualist claim to split, it is reputedly philosophically unilateral in the bad sense – abstract break, lacking sense of the whole and unity – from persecution and the holocaust, these are interpretations of absolute forgetting/withdrawal from the One peculiar to totality and unities; (b) from the heretical point of view which demands it as an autonomous essence having every form implicating bi-laterality and reversibility. This unilaterality is quite distinct from the alterity of the Other. It is that kind of break that we call the *Other than . . .*, and not the *Other of . . .*, and which is heresy itself.

The autonomy of the parts in relation to the Whole, of minorities before the State, of singularities before History, of beings before Being, etc., all of these can only be symptoms of a the heretical decision but cannot replace it. Difference certainly produces the multiple, it is even its crowning glory. But its multiples or multiplicities, without being subsumed under a universal, are identified with them or reconstruct a *superior* universal. And yet the heretic is a individual who does not claim to value universally in that way, by co-extension, intention or intensity, but to force from a unilaterality what the 'singularity' has already recovered. The paradigm of difference must thus be excluded from it also by the introduction of heresy into philosophy or by introducing philosophy to heresy. Contrasting the heretical style with the differential style is contrasting unilaterality with dispersivity [*dispersivité*] and identity with singularity.

Heresy is not reducible to number [*ne fait pas nombre*], surprisingly, and so we must all the more understand why since it forms a multiplicity [*fait multiplicité*]. It has its own 'logic' that avoids the combination of unity and duality and does not form any trinity. Its 'consistency' is that which, no longer being demarcated from logic, is determined-in-the-last-identity by the inconsistency of the Real as cause. It is a thinking according-to-Identity *that it does not give up even when it speaks of transcendence, the multiple, Being, or the Other.* But that frozen thought of Identity is equally a unilateral duality, without these two traits overlapping themselves in a synthesis or system. So Identity does not give rise to a monism and duality does not give rise to a dualism, which are each time abstract constructions or 'in themselves', such as philosophy in setting up the element of an *ultimate transcendental operative which* it gives itself without noticing and without bringing about integration. In approximate terms, *the 1 remains 1 even when it conditionally exchanges itself with the 2, and the 2 remains 2, or 1 in-the-final-identity, without making 3,* it is about the explicit 3 that represents the World of theologico-philosophical Hell, or the implicit 3 as operative background for all philosophies, even the most dualist. More rigorously the One is not the arithmetical 1 and the unilateral Duality is not the 2. Heresy, not being a transcendental arithmetic like philosophy, does not go to the point of the 3 and denies itself continuing beyond the 2. Heresy is thus paradoxically not the choice *of . . .* but the choice *according to* radical Identity rather than the decision on account of singularity.

The heretic really is the only thinker who happens not in the World but in a background. We understand why heresy (even historical heresy) is a decision of an irreducible and incomprehensible kind to metaphysics and theology. It is a decision in favour of that which never had a unique edge or side without ever folding and returning on itself, thus of a completely other structure than the World and History. It is a decision which is no longer included in an ordinary Whole, but that makes itself 'against' the Whole or the mixture. When do heresies begin? With the apparently impossible decision of downgrading the Whole, of depreciating the Church, the State, the World, and History, stripping them of their authority and power. The heretical decision is this historically impossible gesture and nonetheless real.


DUALYSIS, CRITIQUE, DECONSTRUCTION


Heresy is 'in-One' and must be introduced into philosophy, as philosophy is 'in-crisis' and 'in-unrest' and must be introduced to heresy.

In an irreversible way this non-monism (by identity) and non-dualism (by unilateral duality) change Christian dogmas and Gnostic images, concepts and myths. From this ensues devastating effects in religion and philosophy, even when they are 'constructive' and innovative. It possibly returns a new kind of critique of philosophy. Heresy neither overtakes nor does it interiorize onto-theo-logy (either *überwinden* or *verwinden*) in order to bring it to its 'end', but it draws from it non-philosophical and non-theological identities by a special operation called 'cloning'. The concept of critique is assigned to the Real rather than the Rational, to the final-identity rather than sufficiency. Its object is changed, it is transcendence in its greatest extension and its philosophical intensification, it is Unity itself rather than presence, representation, metaphysics, alienation, all concepts of the old critique. Its destructive charge is no longer properly speaking 'critical', 'revolutionary' or 'deconstructive'. For example, through gnosis, heresy has Greek roots among others, but, as theoretical programme, we find it here against the Greco-Christian idealism of the Absolute or auto-divided Unity and of its postmodern modes like Difference. If the foundational gesture of philosophy, that of double transcending in relation to being, can no longer ground heresy, on the other hand these can, without deciding on philosophy, determining it in its ultimately inaccessible identity.

Finally we find in heresy a still unexploited possibility for a dualysis of philosophy as a tradition of the thought-world, a dualysis that has several precisely unilateral *aspects*. It rejects the tragic spirit, the grief of tearing that which is congenital in metaphysics and which does not lead to a practice. It possesses an aspect of deconstruction, but one which subordinates it to determination by the Real. It is a supplementary aspect to philosophy, but it makes of that supplement an identity which is no longer itself supplementary. It is an affirmative aspect as metaphysical will, but it limits the affirmation to an identity cloned by the Real and not to a simulacrum where philosophy dissolves. It is a totalizing aspect of the World, but it only obtains that effect by an Identity that does not belong to that totality-World. It is an aspect of simulating philosophy and theology, but it extracts from these clones rather than simulacrums that are the implosion of philosophical and theological appearance and that can only have reality from the denial of the Real. The strength of heresy, that which rouses prosecution and crime, is its hyper-spiritual abstraction, moreover its being-abstract-without-abstraction, its inconsistency promoted to the rank of necessary but sufficient cause, the absence that is without absence-of-principle and worse than philosophical nothingness and Jewish an-archy, closer to mystical nothingness as is suggested in expressions like Man-in-Man or One-in-One, but without truly merging them with it.


### FROM JEWISH ELECTION TO HERESY


The heretical choice challenges not only the philosophical choice, but also (although to a lesser degree) Jewish election of self by the Other as absolutely Other and its infinity of separation. The principle of this is hyperbolic transcendence, without ontological mediations, as a paradoxical 'performativity' of the Other signified itself in self. An evidently contradictory formula – election is radical heteronomy and takes me hostage. But it also makes me One or a self. And yet the responsibility of myself for the Other, which appears unilateral, extends to the responsibility of the Other for me and in a way envelops it, *such that this Judaism, even the most extreme and rigorous, casts to its periphery the convertibility of self and Other but cannot eliminate it from its own structure and conserve it as constitutive, albeit displaced.* The 'Most-High-Other' [*Très-Hautre*], if we can call it that, could no longer do so in its struggle against the Greek spirit of convertibility. My election by God is nevertheless somewhat my responsibility, the choice is traversed by transcendence and does not reach to a being-separated which would have the primacy of the Real over all separation. Even under this original form, Judaism, which limits the philosophical mixtures with the razor of an infinite transcendence, can only limit them. It oscillates from the autonomy to the heteronomy of choice without being able to conceive it, certainly not as performativity, but as Performed-without-performance. Wanting to avoid unity and scission, philosophical difference, it blames transcendence and indirectly reinforces difference, re-introducing at the heart of the apparatus which had eliminated it. It aggravates the impossibility of choice by removing any performed character from it. *The Jew is a heretic in philosophy, not outside of it. He can interrupt the course of philosophy enough*

*to reverse it and to turn it upside down, not to seize it in its human identity and
its non-sufficiency.*

With the 'Otherwise than being' (Levinas) Judaism brings the
particular to the One as absolute or infinite which short-circuits the
universal, and holds it in place of the universal. Heresy also approaches
the One, but as One-in-One and not as Absolute or as Other. Rather,
it abandons that as its cause and thereby suspends the sufficiency of
the Logos. The most extreme abstraction is common to both Judaism
and heresy, it is sometimes necessary as a break repelling Being and
inhibiting Logos, sometimes as a cause determining the thought of
the World such as it understands Being and Logos. Because heresy
thinks according to the One-in-One, and thinks the World rather
than particularity and singularity, it gives itself the Identity of the
universal, whereas a universal becoming-Jew is a contradiction in
terms, this would not be a classical philosophical absolutization that
puts up with a purge of historical content. Judaically exacerbating the
nothingness of the creation or even dialectically repeating it merely
simulates the gnosis that refuses to place the creature in the World or
in Nothingness.

Universalizing the Shoah, in order to return to it, as is done here, is
especially not, therefore, generalizing it in extension or in comprehension, reducing it to other crimes of history, or making an excuse
out of it. The generalization is revisionist and sometimes negationist,
it has the effect of levelling and undifferentiating crimes, of drowning
their identity and not only their singularity in the generalities of
conscience, culture, history, ideology. From this point of view the
extermination of heretics has nothing to envy elsewhere in the
others and even distinguishes itself in a theoretically interesting
way by its historically, politically and theologically systematic
character. As for the techniques of that extermination, they combine the spiritual and material technologies of the Church, the
theoretical methods of the philosophers, and finally the processes
of all political regimes against their opponents. But above all the
anti-heretic prosecution has invented the *initial solution*, the quasi-
immediate extermination, deferring just the necessary time to
apprehend the Enemy and to travel the reflexive arc of auto-
defence. It is not certain that one can do this better and more
intelligently in the crime against humanity.

## THE TWO SOURCES OF HERESY

One tends to confuse heresy and sect in general. Historico-religious heresies indeed often end by separations, by individual and rebel decisions that cut themselves off from the Whole or from the Body of the Church, from secessions and dissidents who claim to reform values, from powers and dominant dogmas, challenging the strength of a legitimacy and a 'catholicity' that they judge to be usurped anyway

But these separations are only 'reasonable' and 'motivated' in the best of cases, they still postulate a reason – a *Principle of Sufficient Religion* – and thus on the whole go back into the denominational game, but with a different scale of relations between power and dogmas, more micro-political and micro-dogmatic but all the more generally fanatic and obsessional. It is the category of the *heretico-religious*, a vast sphere full of mixtures which range from quasi- to under-churches, sometimes simple 'confessions', which respect these values and like to think of them right away as universals, not particulars or singulars, in the sects founded on the objective of particularity, of micro-gathering and rejection, on the manipulation not only of spirits [*esprits*], as in all churches, but of minds [*esprits*] by way of the body for the ends of money and sex. However, the micro-social or micro-political aspect of sects, let us say it right now reserving the explanation, is only a well-founded objective appearance but is not their final word. A better analysis of the sufficiency of religion and above all the church-form shows that it can form a system with a globalization [*mondialisation*] and a multi-national activity.

If we distinguish heresy and sect, the Identity-without-unity of the former and the closed micro-unity of the latter, the heretical multitudes and the sectarian multiplicities, this will be in order to set the sects and historical heresies on the religious side and oppose them to heresy as Identity-without-principle or the Without-essence. This type of distinction does not result from an analysis but from a dualysis. It does not dissolve the reality of the heretico-religious mixture in its terms, which can only be seemingly opposed but it assumes one term, heretical Identity, separated from its *mixture* with the other (and not from the other himself), and places them in a relation called unilateral duality. The 'great' dominant religions and their sub-groups are on the whole indeed that which we call (unitary) mixtures, not only of 'cross-breedings' but complexes in multiple dimensions (philosophical, political, economic, etc.). On the other hand we call heresy not a unitary form or even a dissident of church and religion, but that which does not have such a social and dogmatic form precisely because it does not base itself on any form or essence, but that it is a radical Identity without consistency of the church and dogma, domination and belief. Heresy is not a principle opposed to that of sufficient Church but a cause-without-principle, an immanent human cause that suspends the Principle of Religion, which is to say the principle by definition. It does not claim *to reform or even to subvert* those truths it supposes or gives itself as universals, thus they only have the appearance of and are 'catholics' only by hallucination and transcendental illusion, but to practically transform them by dualysis.

The heretical subject is only authorized by itself, except that, as subject, it is determined-in-the-last-identity by the human Without-consistency. It contents itself with the exercise of a practice which does not overflow it but does not confuse itself with its existence as separated individual or subject. The individual has its autonomy in its immanent cause and does not hold it in its separation from a Whole that supposes itself legitimate and existent in this way. The authority of the heretical subject (the Christ-subject) is the effect of *an immanent and thus heteronomous cause*. We will carefully distinguish the heretico-religious category where the sectarian is brought in and that of the heretical properly so-called. A sect cannot make a 'heretical cause', a sect diverts heresy from its meaning and again dooms it to the tasks of church and dogma, just socially transgressive, less legitimate but still operating. The spirit of heresy can begin by animating a sect, but cannot be reduced to this and produces other effects, from the practice of dualysis, on the heretico-religious mixture.

## THE SECTARIAN OR HERETICO-RELIGIOUS CATEGORY

The proliferation of sects accompanies a certain destruction or marginalization, a certain loss of legitimacy for the great social and religious unities that are its object, they are their product of decomposition, they reproduce on a miniature scale, micro-religious, the principles of unitary religions. A sect is an anarchic but authoritarian remnant of a large socio-religious entity and, by its destination or end, it only distinguishes itself from that totality in order to identify itself again with a principle of the same kind. The sectarian is an attempt to form a new church, with consequently universal pretensions, on the basis of a particularity and to form the individual in its historical particularity such that it coincides without mediation with an assumed universal that is also affected by a historical particularity. The sectarian multiplicities are in fact individuated by identifications transcendent to a personalized principle, indeed to a person, innumerable 'historical' saviours or messiahs who give themselves afterwards a self-proclaimed divine dimension. Hence the always heteroclite character of sectarian syntheses, too deliberate and calculated, the original fault of real identity and the call resolved in the very worst ways of manipulation and forcing. The heretical duality, being artificially affirmed in a voluntarist and exclusive way, always risks being eliminated, the sect changes into the form of a new church whose claims assure the re-unification by way of exclusion. Undoubtedly the primacy of the individual is already announced, but in a way destined to fail, over the socio-religious totalities. But whereas the subject draws its authority only *as itself in the nearby Real*, it hands over that specific authority in the service of universal truths or dogma, of those that Churches or States provide, and sometimes against the latter.

Heresy and sect were sometimes merged and actually still merge in world-history, but we must learn to distinguish them by their constitution or essence and not only by their evolution. Heresy in its most human essence is the constitution of a transcendental multitude of Christ-subjects, it means, but only because of its account, the positive refusal, without remainder, of these unities, the suspension of the *Principle of Sufficient Church*. Evidently nothing is simple in history, to know that sects can give birth to the spirit of heresy, but also renew these in religions, social forms or unitary and totalized visions of the world. From this point of view most heresies and perhaps all of them have by definition failed not historically but in changing history, and have done so under these two forms which are their destruction, by refocusing or re-unification as micro-religions (it matters in this point of view to distinguish the heretic and the micro-religious, often confused), by their pure and simple destruction by unitary religion.

The spirit of heresy is thus something other than these tests or attempts. How do we develop its charge of unilateral duality against the subjection of human beings to church-thought? By dualysing the heretico-religious mix, without simply claiming to separate them. However, it must not be the remainder of an operation of division, it is autonomous like the human Real itself which draws its causality and legitimacy from its essence of Without-essence rather than in God, or from Thought, Being, Substance, Desire, History, etc. The spirit of heresy (along with the program that follows) has always been mixed, 'forgotten' in and by metaphysics and onto-theo-logy. It is a matrix or a transcendental force that does not manifest itself directly in history as heretico-religious, but only by its effects which are altered from the religious, including here the sectarian, as a symptom, material and model of heresy. It is not 'implicated' or affected by the effects that it produces there. Heresy is not therefore only a theory and practice, in history, of parts, factions and small groups as irreducibly multiple and refusing to return under Unity, Totality or the Universal. It is the theory and practice only of individuals or of uni-lateralities to the exclusion of every assumed universal. The primacy of parts over the Whole is therefore a formula that demands to be clarified, as conversely the micro-ecclesiological character of sects.

## CHURCH, SECT, OVER-CHURCH: THE PRINCIPLE OF SUFFICIENT CHURCH

A new labyrinth embarrasses the reason of the human sciences, it is this question of sects. It is understood by the precariousness of the criteria of empirical or 'material' distinction when it claims a the-oretical value as is the case in these sciences and the intellectual debates. Our object is not how to distinguish empirically religions and sects, rather a demand for our material. We allow the sociologists and the intellectuals, as well as believers, to add to the necessary complexity of this question. The material criteria are fragile and weak, churches and sects always resort, in the long term of their history, to the same procedures of exploitation and mental, sexual and financial manipulation to different degrees of cynicism, stupidity and deadly cruelty, which does not allow them to oppose them one to another in a sure way. We have attempted to say that the sects explain all means by their end, which is to exist or, in other words, to dominate and to exploit. But this criterion is a little general and belongs to the religions, above all to the least mild. The similarity of functioning, of coercive procedures and of criminality between sects and the 'great society', sometimes of the 'great church', have been sufficiently raised in order to render them indiscernible, not to say identical, at least in the long historical process. The sectarian pathology has nothing to envy in those churches or recognized religions that conceal their past nor in the effects of the 'uneasiness of civilization' in which it is concentrated. The notion of societies and, we will add, of churches as 'global sects', at least has the validity of a central theme for these problems, and moreover the affinity of sects, financial circuits and data processing, the Idea of a sectarian web. Internet users are the followers or believers betrayed in the fantasy of space and universal communication that shows the completely reticular form which can capture belief, that is to say, transcendence.

However, the radical heretical point of view has some effect on these unstable distinctions. The previous short remarks remain interior to the heretico-religious sphere. But the most operational distinction, the most manipulability is that which opposes and connects, in that same sphere, the churches (rather than the religions) and the sects. It is a stronger criterion, formal or 'transcendental' as the philosophers would say, thus the sociologists give a weakened version, but which touches on the same form of the phenomenon. A church is a group of procedural powers which have the property of unitarily or hierarchically federating diverse confessions or sub-unities, of conceiving a development or a coherent variation of its forms and dogmas, eventually interiorizing and integrating certain sects. The sect creates dissidence from its particularity and definitively closes up on a community *which accepts no sub-component* and on dogmas which are affirmations without becoming. Even if the sects have a tendency to form multinational spheres of influence under the cover of grand ideas like the struggle against communism or against capitalism, for the spiritualization of the world and an evangelical globalization, and through complete-education, complete-legality, complete-finance, that distinction is less empirical than the theoretical usage that is ordinarily made, it is constitutive of the *difference* of church and sect. Its sense does not stop at the effect of 'difference', empirically badly understood, or from simple opposition. Because difference is more complex than simple opposition, it is also a correlation and reversibility, with or without exchange. Every difference is relative and absolute and signifies a co-belonging of the church-form and the sect-form, their indissociability even in their reciprocal hatred. Hence their affinity in the processes of human subjugation, their common end. *And yet this common end in every church and every sect is supported by a universal factor that we will call 'over-church', which is the vehicle of the Principle of Sufficient Church in the churches where it puts itself at risk, and in the sects where it withdraws on the particularity.* There is no church or sect without this over-church factor open to two seemingly contrary destinies. The sectarian secession, which is based on a deception of the faithful concerning validity or an ancient cult, co-belongs to the churches or presupposes them, a large part of their activity being the limitation and inhibition of forces of uncontrolled rupture. The churches are triumphant and live through the difficulties of triumphs and, thus closing their eyes, intentionally insist on the sectarian unilaterality, on the unchecked and dangerous renewal of their forms and dogmas. In this sense the sects are the internal problem of the churches, their point of interrogation.

The churches are only the inverse of the system, the overtaking and interiorization of sects when they are not the old pagan identifications. The churches are sects which have achieved and completed their movement, which have been known to redeploy the *continued separation* of the sect as a *being-separate* now articulated and dominated. The sects are churches that have failed or most often apparently decided to fail and to grow, by continued separation, in secret and obscurity, continuing the same end of general exploitation of human subjects as the churches but in forms that are most triumphant at their birth. Finally the over-church is a unitary tendency to universality and unicity that rules as much in the church, where it exposes itself and becomes dull at the same time, as in the sect, where it is most virulent and repellent. The over-church factor brings together the separation and the separated and is expressed par excellence in the Roman Catholic Church which makes itself out to be universal, unique and prototypical – it is the victory of the Sufficient Church. Given this kind of definition, the Reformation has given place to a genuine church federating a multitude of denominational sub-groups, even if it has literally begun as a sect via a separation, an ambiguity that Catholics have tried their to best to maintain with the term 'separated brothers', playing on sectarian *separation*, which remains a continuation, and the *separated* who turn the separation into the church and which removes the original sect. In conclusion, what apart from societies and churches practices a sectarian consumerism and what sectarian folly exasperates these urges other than the societies and churches striving to overcome them?

Compared with the church-sect-overchurch system, more interesting than the indeterminate Idea of religion, radical heresy is abstract but is not the result of an abstraction, whereas the sect is a continued abstraction. It is a being-separated but one which, unlike that which passes for it in the church, does not result from a prior separation against a Whole or a Federation and is not destined to be reconciled with the separation. It is thus not born of a sect but to the contrary eventually brings it to life in a unilateral manner. Nothing is more opposed than the sectarian spirit and the spirit of heresy, one is closed and locked inside itself and the other transforms what little opening there is in the church itself, not through a supplementary opening waiting to be shut again and closed in on itself, but by a cause that definitively determines it in the being-open or future.

### FOR A CHURCH-SUBJECT OR ORGANON: AGAINST THE PRINCIPLE OF SUFFICIENT SACRAMENT

The interminable war of sects, Churches and States in the confused name of the rights of the person or the good of man, of secularity [*laïcité*] or liberty, gives way to a mess, inextricable from determinations and causalities. It feeds the 'debates' of intellectuals who love to make these twists and turns and play one against the other. What does it provide besides the intellectuals? For heretics it is grist for the mill that will make the material useful for struggle. The problem for heretics is that of 'the extension of struggle', being the old politico-economic revolution, to a complex object that they call the 'World' and where economics, politics, religion, law, etc. are merged so that equally universal attributes overlap and mutually control themselves indefinitely. There is a politics of sects that is economic, racist, globalist, etc., and it can only grow. The World is here, a determination among many others, the tendentially indiscernible character of the churches and sects in the form of multiplicites of fusions, circles of influence and diversely rigid kinds of obedience, that rigidity follows, from the excuse that binds and controls humans as animals, according to the totalitarian argument of Nietzsche, the foreclosure of Man-in-person as subject. This new struggle, really universal, is no longer the concern of intellectuals and must be able to theoretically 'dominate' its object. The struggle is that of subjects who will finally have the means of no longer confusing their object with their practice, heresy precisely refuses to let them reciprocally determine each other. It is this practice of unilateral duality that allows, for example, the introduction among the means of struggle those objectives called 'law-and-order' [*sécuritaires*] and 'prophylactics' formerly reserved only for the sects and that must be extended, with this expressed reservation, to the churches themselves.

As for the Church, in the measure where it is still discernible in the heretico-religious mess, it is not necessary to reject it as an infernal Babylon, for its concept may also be dualysed. There is no necessity to choose between the dominant Church, subjugation by dogmatic and authoritative infallibility, and the servant Church, developing a 'self service' of individual beliefs. From these two extremes, which make a circle, we unilaterally distinguish the Church-subjector organon. It varies like the former in terms of the beliefs that create circumstances, occasions or arguments, but is invariant like the latter, not only in its dogmatic an institutional materiality, which equally creates circumstances, but in its ultimately human identity, and thus, in a sense certainly not Catholic, 'infalliable' such that it unilaterally determines these variations.

Two sufficient conceptions must be avoided, the sacralization and the instrumentalization of the church, which must remain a *transcendental organon determined by the invariant of Man-in-person*. The duty of the subject is not that of Man, the church is not a servant in that general or unitary sense, and no more than it is dominating and legislating. To the duty of the single subject, merging with him, it ceases to alienate the Man-in-Man and is no longer instrumentalizable as if it were an indefinitely intensified tool and a tool for tools in a circuit of implementality [*ustensilité*] and reciprocal service. That dualysation of the church allows, against a symbolic impoverishment, for the introduction of rites and sacraments but limits their scope in their non-dogmatic capture by removing from them the unitary pretension of the sacraments which is the same as that of divine sufficiency, and this from baptism in particular which concerns only the subject and not Man-in-person. Against the sufficient sacrament, we will put forward the sacrament-organon. This is not just a simple 'instrument' of grace nor a work of men in general, it is identically an instrument of subjects or of their works, but determines in-the-last-identity by that grace that gives and does not cease giving, Man-in-person. It is not the place of any church to give a verdict on Man-in-person, to bestow upon or refuse him a 'kingdom'. He alone determines in-the-last-identity, as the non-decisional subject (of) self, the meaning of the church and sacraments as organon. That is the theorem that solves the paradox of this conception and marks the destruction of the Principle of Sufficient Church, *the church-subject is autonomous or authorises itself by itself in its final nearly human determination*. It is the Christ-church, finally.

## HERETICAL DUALITY AGAINST DUALISM

Dualism has received a metaphysico-religious form in history. It begins by recognizing the superior authority in the principle of the One and by distinguishing it from a second principle with which it is mixed. But it is precisely dualism, when it takes this form, that contents itself with asserting the One in a transcendent manner (beyond Being or the World), as Unity or Unicity. It is therefore a simple religious concept or one which puts up with contradiction, because Unity always absorbs duality. Being that these two principles are posed from the mode of transcendence and exclusion/interiorization, the second is finally subordinated to the first, reducible to it by way of complicated mechanisms that Iranian and Syrian dualism have elaborated. Dualism is always imbalanced and has monist tendencies.

One axiom of this essay is that true duality, that which is irreducible to metaphysical Unity, is not dualism but assumes that the 'first principle' is the One as separated by immanence from Being and from every form of unity. It then *leaves Being* a 'second principle' which will be the autonomous possibility of evil and mixture. Duality is properly that 'of principles', except that the One is not a principle, and consequently the other side is that of principles, that is to say of the Principle of Sufficient Philosophy. *Duality of the Without-principle and of the Principle, that is the key to the most radical heresy, which is not dualism exactly.* The effect of unilateral duality is to dissolve for its own sake or that of the Christ-subjects, the mixtures that form the substance of evil, when at least they like to think of themselves as the Real, and how could they not want this? Starting with two principles, nothing more, and by the mode of transcendence and exclusion, we give these a religious and theological interpretation as in the Gnostic dualisms which are all religious, and we bring it into a contradiction that throws up these unbearable traditional dualisms. Hence their pretention to immediately dissolve reality into a mixture by isolating one from the other of the two principles whose mixture is evil. This is a contradiction owing to two correlative traits:

1. the One is understood via the mode of the superior Unity and transcendent in relation to the World;
2. the second principle is understood as being purely itself (via the mode of pure evil = absolute) and not as mixture, but as the principle of mixture in which it implicates the first.

We have proposed, if we can say it this way, to destroy the contradiction of these religious dualisms (which precisely ground sects and which only come under the heretico-religious category). Thereby the two principles are revised. Non-Christian heresy is neither the rather monist Syro-Egyptian kind, (the first principle is not here the origin of the second, the vision-in-One does not engender the World by emanation, division, etc.), nor is it in fact the Iranian and Manichean type (the two co-eternal principles are not mixed together, but the

World is already every possible mixture and the vision-in-One clones the Christ-subject from the World without mixing it with itself). Nothing is divine – Man is 'in-Man' – and there is only one principle, the World, but it is the principle of principles, the capacity [*puissance*] of principles, of dominations and sub-dominations. As principle of principles, philosophy is an archontology, an onto-archaeo-logical difference which dualyses non-philosophy. We specify it thus:

1.   Absolute and pure evil as a principle is a religious and transcendent conception. We oppose to it a (second) principle which is no longer pure or unmixed evil, but mixture itself. Thus human existence does not develop *at the heart of* some evil-mixture, which is no longer an exterior or interior principle, menacing and diabolical, but *a necessary condition or occasion of its existence as Christ-subject.* Against its religious interpretation, the evil-mixture is here restored as that which Western meta-physics has always considered as being its superior principle, Being, which is precisely a mixed notion, the mixture of transcendence and immanence. There will be no two principles into which evil is decomposed, but one alone, evil itself as mixture par excellence. The true non-contradictory duality is between a principle that is already mixture and another (principle) that eludes every mixture and thus forbids any reconstitution of a unity, of a unifying monism.

2.   Neither philosophy nor religion have ever correctly conceived of the One as distinct by immanence from Unity. The essence of the One makes it necessary to think it as alien [*étrangère*] to every consistency or transcendence. The One is radically inherent (in) the One as Indivision and experiences itself [*s'éprouve*] through a specific mode. Hence the exclusion of nothingness, reflection, division, etc., and a complete reversal of perspective in relation to metaphysics. This is not the One which must be conceived as non-Being but, since the One is Immanent-in-person and thus the Separated, it is Being or evil which must be conceived as not (-One) but affected by (non-)One or by unilaterality. This Being-mixed must be dualysed as a mode of those two forms that are claimed in general to be 'non-One'.

The path of metaphysical and Gnostic dualism to the really determined transcendental duality is what alone allows for the liquidation of Unity as a principle common to metaphysics, religion, and their Gnostic modes. This immanent and transcendental duality implicates the displacement of classic duality, which ceases to be that of two principles in order to become that of Immanence-in-person and transcendence in-Immanence. The duality now orders the One and diverts it without continuity, but the One is no longer itself one of these two principles, taken in the encompassing self-enclosure that still tolerates dualism. It is as if we had measured the traditional dualism of gnosis in terms of the vision-in-One that determines-in-the-last-identity, the monism of Being and of dualism.

THINKING 'FICTION'

The determinations of heresy in that which it can have as universal are no longer simple philosophical concepts. Their investment in the field of faith is problematic and calls for some protocols. They are ultimately unlearned [*indoctes*] things in the sphere of Christianity, some creedal-tools [*outils-symboles*]. No longer philosophizing faith and dogmas, it is not inversely about Christianizing philosophy, of redoing the work already done under the form of innumerable theologico-philosophical mixtures unlike the end of heresy which is to subtract them in their sufficiency from mixture by producing their human Identity. A 'unified theory of Christianity and heresy' in the person of the Future Christ implements these creedal-tools within a certain diverse doctrine of Christianity, Gnosticism and Judaism. A heretical practice of concepts and dogmas? This is not quite what the common sense of the philosopher can hear in the expression. Heresy is here symbolized and formalized in a *quasi-* conceptual way and extracted from its religious savagery and fantasies. The authority and mechanisms of philosophy are, as those of theology and the Church, definitively displaced and restricted in the World. That unilateral axis of Man-without-world and World is heresy and substitutes itself for philosophical and theological difference, which will however rediscover there a place but one for material of thought. God himself still has a final function to carry out, a final chance to understand, and his lot is neither worse nor better than those Great Personages of philosophy: Being, Other, One. As for Judaism, and at its most irreducible core, it also directs him towards the problem of the victim and finds an exceptional place for a *witness for the prosecution in the disagreement between Man and the World.*

Heresy, in its universal concept, that which is not acquired by generalization and extension of religious and philosophical phenomena, *is a practice 'performed-without-performation' thus in-the-last-identity rebelling* against the World, but in a theoretical, and not theoreticist, nature in its subject and material. It is in this practice that the possibility of a universal fiction in philosophical material takes root, founded upon cloning rather than on the imagination. The religious forms of heresy, gnosis, had only the ontological instrument of philosophy at their disposal so they compensated for this inadequacy with a profusion of myths and for which they were often reproached and came to swell the record of indictments. These religious myths are now at our complete disposal in view of a philo-fiction, begun by gnosis itself but through which we can produce more elaborate resources.

Philosophers can be polemicists, heremeneutes, preachers, workers, poets, doctors, legislators, jurists, all sorts of diverse styles that provide colour for the concept and to which we should add diatribe, apologetic, psychedelic patchwork, etc. By right heresy thus uses all these styles, adding to them for example hymn and aphorism, and also prayer, but under modification, as so many *aspects* of its discourse that turns them from exhorted transcendence to determined transcendence. It is not impossible to consecrate to the One-in-One as Man the methods of a hymn of gratitude and adoration or the style of a prayer, subject to their axiomatic and theoretical transformation. The heretic must resolve a specific problem which is only with him – the removal of the discourses of transcendence and faith, of logic and hope as material for a cloning producing knowledge. Heresy is less a total knowing disguising a philosophical faith than a theory determined by an unlearned knowing.

A characteristic of the heretical style, a feature of gnosis under an imaginative and mythological form, is already a variety of materials for thought. Precisely because the material is contingent or secondary and has neither the primacy of Man-in-Man nor the priority of the heretical subject, it accepts a certain liberty in choice, but which can give the impression of a syncretism to which philosophy immediately opposes the system. However, we distinguish the rigourous heretical practice, determined according to a cause, informed by the rules which are invariant but susceptible to diverse content or applications, and a religious syncretism as so many doctrines are, without speaking of philosophical mixtures. The rigour of universal heresy is, in its manner, both that of a science in consideration of cases, rules, procedures, and by the necessary reference to the data of experience, that of a philosophy in relation to that World that a transcendental Christ-subject assumes, and finally that of a fiction from the liberty of decisions, the work on language and the imagination of its formulations, but it is not that of philosophy normalized or rigidified in the war of particular positions.

It is regardless an acceptable task, not a regression, for introducing within a certain theoretical mastery, radically limited as well, old religious and other themes that belong to the thought-world and that can rise to the condition of an object for a rigorous discipline finally determined by Man-in-Man. If one wishes to name the historical conditions of thought, in our assumed post-metaphysical situation, we can estimate that after so much pretension and sufficiency that do not concern themselves with man except to manage his alienation, a bet may be made on the simply human, but unexploited, pertinence of heresy and on the possibility of introducing to it an adequate form of conceptualization. Raised to a 'concept', heresy itself frees itself from these heteroclite religious forms. Thus, there will not be a new 'heretical faith', but a plain use of a great thought buried by history.


## OF UTOPIA AS ASCETICISM AND RESISTANCE

Heresies are the research and practice of a utopia, and the radical heresy of the Man-in-person is the discovery of the Real as *determinate* utopia. Utopia is not always a delirium of the imagination, it can also be a radical poverty of representations, determining more profoundly an imagination and fiction that change life, which *express* the Living-without-life such as it determines life. What will a life be according to utopia and heresy? Without simply denying them, invalidating their sufficiency, it will make by means of conformism – obedience and project, faith and dogma, consent and renunciation – the methods of liberation for the subject which is to say its constitution as Future Christ.

'Future Christianity' is life's birth in the spirit of heresy against all of its conservative revivals and restorations. Awakening them to faith, the modernization of dogma and their placement within the taste of the day is no more the business of heresy than is the 'renewal of thought' from out of the 'end of philosophy'. Heresy is not a solution erupting in a space freed by philosophy and religion. Regardless, the latter two practise the occupation of soil and spaces right into their 'death' and turn away any who would bury the heretics there. Heresy is utopic, it is not even a story 'in the heavens' rather than in the World. It comes into existence with Man-in-Man as ultimately resistant without-place (without World) and without-time (the 'radical past'), non-heroical resistant to philosophical heroism. Undoubtedly there is no use for Man-in-person but by the subject in the World, it is thus up to the subject to make use of the World and to deliver himself from his enchantment.

Here it is the real that 'makes' heresy, heresy is the innocence of Man, undoubtedly because it is not completely a metaphysical animal, which is to say an animal. The *will* of heresy is a will like any other and a form of idealism. As far as we understand it, this is not a doctrinal position though, barely a programme, a posture rather, an asceticism or a poverty of spirit. Heresy is not a point of view or a vision of the World since it is not thought which would want to be 'heretical' at the risk of returning to a heresy proper to the religious sphere. Refuse to fill in this poverty with Being, the Multiple, Affectivity, Language or Text, Mathematics or any other science. Remain in the Without-essence of the One, do not fill it in with God, do not flee into faith. The spirit of non-sufficiency, more ontic than ontological, shakes off the world but can give only it. The asceticism is not necessarily the *ascetic ideal*, it is Immanence-in-person rather than

Nothingness, asceticism in-the-final-identity capable of determining a new life. Asceticism is no longer here an idealized process but a being-separated that engages thought in ways alien to philosophy and to metaphysical drunkenness. Whether heresy from the One or from Man-in-person, what results from it for the World? How do we make heresy something other than an adjective – a first name that liberates religious language from religion and the word of faith from faith?

## NOTES

1  In Gnosticism 'Eon' (also spelled 'Aeon') designates a divine power or nature emanating from the Supreme Being and playing various roles in the operation of the universe. Hans Jonas notes that the various eons that populate the various forms of Gnosticism are equivalent to the Gnostic understanding of 'World' that a subject finds himself lost within, the sense of World Laruelle plays with here. Jonas also notes that Eon brings together the temporal and spatial into a quasi-personal power that one must go through in order to reach the ultimate goal of salvation. See Hans Jonas (2001), *The Gnostic Religion: The Message of the Alien God and the Beginnings of Christianity* (Boston: Beacon Press), pp. 51–54.

2  Laruelle is making a play on words here that is untranslatable. He is playing on the question of the 'in(-one) and the we(-beings)' mentioned above by making this the same question of the Gnostic 'Eon'. We have chosen to give both the French and the English translation. Note that the one of 'in-(one)' is note the same 'one' Laruelle usually makes reference to [l'Un], but the 'one' of the impersonal third-person. The French translation of what is translated as 'the They' in the Macquarrie and Robinson English translation of Heidegger's Being and Time is *l'on*.

3  The ancient Greek word *hairesis* meant 'the act of choosing' and is the noun form of the verb *hairein* which meant 'to take'. According to etymologists, in time the noun developed the extended senses of

'a choice,' 'a course of action,' 'a school of thought,' and 'a philosophical or religious sect.' Stoicism, for example, was a 'hairesis.'

[4] Laruelle is again playing on the ancient Greek *hairesis*. See note above.

[5] Laruelle is here using the French neologism *performation*. I've translated it as a cognate as he is playing with the combination of the ideas of performance and formation and thus performation signifies a formation through performance.

# CHAPTER THREE
## The Past Foreclosed to Memory

THE SUFFICIENCY OF MEMORY AND
HERETICAL ULTIMATION

Defending heresy, renewing it as a simple 'question', demanding it be brought again before the court, this is a trap that stretches the example of anti-Semitic crimes for us. Heretics have earned better than our compassion. It is necessary to defend their memory, but not to think from their memory alone or from the crime of which they have been the object, not to avenge them with an anamnesis, not to go back over an extermination at the risk of dissolving the procession of tragedies in history. Our bad conscience is such that every crime must automatically appear to call for a supposedly sufficient repentance. It would be enough for the memory to keep alive the remembrance of a crime so that the Irreparable can be wiped away or it would suffice to 'justify' its return to the global order of justice and meaning. As if humanity could agree to the forgiveness of crimes that it carried out against itself or God wash away his complicity. We prefer to think anew about a forgiveness as ancient as he who asks for forgiveness. We do not replace theodicy with a mnemodicy. Heresy is the occasion that keeps the crime alive but precisely not in memory, rather it keeps it alive in the state of the radical past as a 'remembering' because it is outside-time and outside-justice but 'justifies' history. Restoring justice for the persecuted is necessary but it is only a half solution. Compassion, the labour or even the duty of memory cannot be the necessary cause for the right of victims nor for a right that does not fortify *in extremis* infamy. The justice of memory or that of repentance is perhaps a *sufficient reason* for the protection of victims, but cannot be its real cause, giving its irreducible reality in the World, preventing it from returning under the law of crime and dissolving there. Justice directed towards the oppressed is necessarily in bad faith, intensifying the crime by its memory and by its faith in the sufficiency of their system. It is a double faith and it is one faith too many.

Heresy is not only Man defined as a victim, rather the victim is the cause which determines the real content of the investigation and instruction. The protection of victims is motivated by philosophy, ethics and law in a manner too short and analytic, directly by the crime itself and its immediate effects, or in a manner too long and synthetic, by the addition of any ideal and theoreticist belief as memory and repentance, or as the exemplarity of sufficient punishment as determining the necessity of the investigation and the sanction for the crime's erasure. All the known solutions find a place between these two extremes, it is said that justice is the business of the World system, of specular self-defence, which is precisely crime as a system of self-sufficiency. But it is impossible to keep the crime alive (which is to say the victim) in the ideal element of memory or confession. They remain as the Lived-without-life, without memory or confession, as what is there (of) the Real that extracts justice-according-to-Man from the 'justice of men' in rendering it unjustifiable by them. The Shoah has progressively invented, not without excess and deviations, its own justice and memory, heresy must invent forms of its own forgetting and memory, which are neither those of Judaism nor of philosophy, infinity of the Other or truth of Being. Man does not forget Man as he forgets the truth of Being, or God, or even his own crimes. In fact he cannot forget Man as the last Identity in-which he thinks, neither can he recall it himself, at most he forgets everything in exercising the thought *according to* . . . that primacy of Man over the World. The crime of crime is to make him forget this by convincing him of its sufficiency.

HERETICAL TIME: FROM THE PAST-IN-MEMORY TO THE
MEMORY-IN-THE-PAST

It doesn't matter, even if this fact is difficult to accept, that the Shoah has been turned into an object of various lucrative activities, that there has been a perverse exploitation by the victims of their own misfortune, or that some speak in an unacceptable way of the holocaust survivors' fabrication and of an ideologico-historical construction. *The symptom* is the only thing that is important, *at least here*, as it allows a work of dualysis or, as Husserl would say in a rationalist context, the imaginary variations that can 'free the essence'.

We have received from the Shoah a certain number of concepts that we now use in a completely different manner as first terms axiomatized from an inventive heretical thought and not only as simple bits of information. These are the past, memory, crime, culpability, revision and negation (revisionism and negationism). Assume the following axioms, accompanied with some comments.

1. The past has not been considered in philosophy as past in-memory (object of memory, saved or repressed by it, identical to it, etc., at best identical to remembrance and a pure memory), thus as past-in-image or in-remembrance. From its perspective memory has been considered as an anthropological faculty or instance, the past and memory in general as functions of a worldly time or even reduced and immanent to consciousness, *always philosophizable or sufficient.*

2. The real past is not representable or in-memory, it is *in-past* or *in-identity* without constituting one in itself, it is *found and experienced only in-past* in its own immanence. The radical past is by definition time as memorial given-without-donation and cannot be forgotten, being itself foreclosed to memory – this no longer means 'forgotten' in the usual or ontological sense. *The in-past is no longer a dimension of time and situated from its turn in a time already surreptitiously supposed, in a behind-time* [arrière-temps] *operative and unobserved as such*. Its reduction to memory, to the image, to pure remembrance and even to the original dimension of retention, are modes of an idealized and theoreticist

representation, of its dissolution in its double, of its *hallucinatory forgetting*.

3.   The real past, unlike the memory-image or the thought-memory, is a past-without-memory, given without an operation of forgetting and anamnesis, foreclosed from memory itself or un-forgotten. It is the unique time, its identity from immanence before it even existed and it is through the material of memory that it can exist, that is it assumes the function of a future subject. It is that which determines memory, but does nothing but determine it. Memory is a function of the thought-world and thought-history, subject to misappropriation and falsification, to historical rectification also. Under that double form it is merely *a material not only to rework as the faith of the historian-philosopher, but to clone by the radical past in a subject-form*, a memory-subject might as well be effectively reworked under that condition.

4.   The immanent or inecstatic past is inexistent and inconsistent but precisely as capable of determining memory and the present as material for the future. This inconsistency in worldly time can determine in the-last-identity a subject-time as future that is also inecstatic (that at which philosophy aims in a symptomal way in the half-solution of temporalist and originary time).

5.   The heretical problem is *par excellence* that of the type of past foreclosed from memory itself and from every anamnesis. From this point of view it is able to transform our relationship to the Shoah, radicalizing its sense of the failure of meaning, returning revisionism and negationism to their complicity with the criminals, at the same time that we remain alert to variations and hesitations of memory's judgement. The past-in-the-past is by definition inalienable in the adventures and misadventures of memory, in its resentment and its culture of bad conscience. And this alone can determine it in-the-last-identity, that which needs to be on pain of returning to its initial complicity with the forces particular to the World of levelling and Conformism. To determine memory by a past-outside-time, *no longer cloning as anamnesis but as future*, this is a heretical task.

6. The history-memory is a representation of the past, its division and its splitting, where it dissolves itself in objective fantasies. It is anonymous and attributable to the men seized in transcendence, collectively or not, in the first person or in every other. On the other hand, the memory-clone, which is no longer split except in its material state but identical-in-the-past or by its cause, which is the future, formed under that which exists finally as subject of the past-in-the-past. Strictly speaking, the radical past does not exist and does not want to pass into existence, but it determines the old time as existant-Future. The subject is not an existant *in* the future but an existant subject from the mode of the future and exhausts itself in it.[1] The time-subject is the existant-Future-time in which it uses the old temporalities of the World, History and religious Myth. It is even about a pragmatic of the memory-world, not of a worldly manipulation of memory. What does it serve to cultivate and work memory if it isn't to 'produce' the dimension, *inecstatic in-the-last-identity*, of a future which transforms the old times 'in transcendence' inhabited by History? Already the 'duty of memory' is unable to signify a closure of memory on itself, rather than a time hyperbolic and 'against time'. Especially the existing-Future happening in a history-time from a past which withdraws from every consistency.

7. The touchstone of philosophy, 'the height' of thought and condescension for men, here over memory as it is elsewhere, is in the horrible discourse of 'ideological victimhood [*victimaire*]', where everyone recognizes the professionals of intellectual courage. It has become unthinkable that 'unhappy memory' can be healed by that therapeutic shopkeeper. Taking memory into account, to compensate for an incontestable calamity by the always narcissistic haphazard occasion of the recognition or work for rectification and adjustment of the historian, that which is called revisionism, though it matters little whether it is philosophical or not. Work and criticism cannot be first, as philosophy wants it to be, for memory as for everything, on pain of lapsing into hermeneutic idle-chatter and a pathetic bad conscience. The *radical evil* of the heretics is a constraint in the shape of a test not just to reform our concept of memory but to save the concept in remembering its identity in the name of the most radical past as it has never been in-memory.

## REVISIONISM 1: MEMORY AND FORGETTING

Form the past as a transcendence that no longer passes to absolutized being, we thus distinguish the past which, from being radical, does not pass in transcendence itself, as we distinguish from the question-without-response the creative [*créatrice*] response to problems. Heresy is a solution that precisely determines the problems as solvable and suppresses the infinite religious urge. On the whole it is that the victim calls into question the effect of philosophy's having given primacy and not just priority to memory over the past itself. It has continued to make of this the result of an operation, incapable of pulling it out of constituted time and, finally, of the World. With the primacy of memory over time and in particular over the past, the reduction of this to the adventures of history and anthropology, it is once again philosophy and its ambiguities that carry it over the past-in-the-past and its temporal-worldly non-consistency. Philosophy's spirit of confusion mixes the past and memory, the one as object of the other, its combinations being possible under the sign of their revers-ibility or their convertibility (aside from some nuances).

Between traces and tasks, resentment and honesty [*propreté*], activity and reactivity like Nietzsche said, memory has become the Western archive of philosophical wanderings and hesitations. Memory also has a history, especially since the Shoah puts it to work and gives it a new impetus. Philosophers and historians have worked in the cracks, through which this living-as-excessive event has interrupted the continuity of history and memory. For example, the duty of memory to be 'revised' in a work of Christian memory, memory's absolute effect by a hermeneutic of its meaning. Regarding the past and memory, those sites where we are given, in an apparently unique way, the Jewish question and the Heretic question, the philosophy of the last century has concentrated itself in the effort to distinguish it from worldly time understood in a narrow way as chrono-logical and temporalized time. But as usual, even among those who suspect its fraudulent use against the Jews or in their favour, it has accepted the reduction of the past to memory. And yet it is there rightly a problematic idealist thesis, because there is no evidence that the experience of the Shoah and especially that of heretics is a matter of memory. Nothing, apart from the customary idealism of philosophy, is therefore allowed to deprive the past of its reality and to reduce it to that of awareness. How is a real event and memory distinguished from what they give place to? It is not about a 'bullish realism' but a problem of justice. Revisionism comes out of philosophical and idealist forms and begins with the negation of certain forms of reality. The small distinction of the direct witness and the historian ends up being laughable, as if the murdered Jews were 'witnesses' to their own murder and bear those kinds of categories. *Victims are never witnesses, good or bad, faithful or not, we cannot be witnesses in a trial, and if the Jews are witnesses it is as survivors in the trial who must follow their murder in an immanent way.* They disrupt the far too often fabricated economy that makes them subjects or objects for historians and philosophers. Can we imagine the murdered victim saying 'it was this way' or even 'I was there'? If they 'were there', it was as humans-in-person who are not in Being or the World, who in a sense *do not exist.* How can one explain the reluctance of those who 'were there' to speak and effectively squander their misfortune under the form of an experience that can be repeated, a discretion that does not always respect the heirs of the Shoah? Can we distinguish the 'living wound' and the memory of the wound, in order to restore the former to the latter and speculate about it as the idealist does? Regarding the living wound, the victim knows the most fatal wound and has little time or strength for the knowledge that he has been sacrificed thus on the altar of philosophy. Wanting to reconcile the crime and historiographies' academic thoughtlessness leading to a reciprocal mediation for which the revisionist levelling of the crime pays for with some conceptual nuances and the historian's 'labour'.

The victims are no longer particulars or like those particularisms in opposition to the 'universality' of philosophers. Yes, they are 'blind' or 'blinded', but it is that which gives their thought force. If the survivors sometimes give themselves up to those attempts at the reappropriation of calamity, that infidelity can give rise to a legitimate irritation but does not legitimate revisionism, even philosophical revisionism. There is obviously some scandal in speaking of victimization as one does about a 'mood', and a theoretical irresponsibility, except in clearly asserting the primacy of the victim over its posterior victimization, which it determines. Philosophy cannot begin except by that originary denial of the Real by representation, it closes its eyes and constructs its thought in an ideal blinding light, but it is not 'blind' like the victims are. In a different way than the historian, he reconstructs a Real of substitution, an image or a memory of reality that splits itself into a 'fact' or 'event', or some other device, and thus he believes to have been made the spokesperson of it by delegation. The 'memory of the Shoah' is an amphibological expression which sweeps away all the revisionisms, from the most specular to the most speculative. Religions and philosophies love history and memory, they maintain a constitutional relationship to the past by their intermediary and *have forgotten the crime in its retelling*. These are some techniques of memory through which recent technologies are made to see antiquity and mythical nature. They are based on that retelling [*rappel*], but the thinking-according-to-the-crime is not a simple reminder [*rappel*] and the Shoah is not our mythology even if it always risks becoming so by means of exclusive identifications. Whether these are history's depth, height or alterity, memory, with its reduced antinomies, forgotten or anamnesis, duty or work, is a procedure of sufficient and softened victimization – and prolongs the crime.

The pertinent distinction is not between the imperative memory as duty and the historical memory as work, which can only fight and encroach on the domain of the other, but between *non-memory, unlearned or immemorial knowledge specific to the victim, which is not a forgetting or anamnesis*, and the diverse practices of memory which nevertheless no longer have to 'digest' the crime but think history according-to-the-crime. Only the crime in its immemoriality or its non-memoriality can determine new uses for forgetting and memory. From that point of view it is heresy which gives its true intelligibility to the Shoah without revising or denying it, asserting to the contrary the right of its demand in asserting its last identity, which does not even exist as the Other still exists.

Heretics in effect are not in existence and do not have any essence, they are not the object of our memory, they are neither 'present' nor 'absent' in the sense that philosophy may intend these words. They are a mode of blinded or unlearned being-given and have no need for being recalled in our remembrance, unable to disappear or be for-gotten. By definition they fall outside the power of the conspiratorial [*machineuses*] faculties of representation. *Heresy is a model of thinking missing from as far back as the origins in so far as is necessary as the Real, out of a non-historical necessity*. In a sense it is our 'last thought', still fully on this side of Being and the Other, our Last Good News, that which gives birth to the empty hope of philosophical and historical salvation. The historical 'forgetting' of heresy is thus absolutely positive in its manner and is witness to a *universality of a past-without-history outside-memory*. The forgetting of forgetting, its dialectic and simplicity, is only the same as Being and its adventures in becoming-memory. To the contrary the heretical in-past is universal under all the possible historical conditions and conjunctures and is as valuable to the Jews as to other men. It is not in any way a pretention to the totalization of human history, simply a negative universal condition of that history. It is as a 'negative' condition that it is necessary to understand that 'missing' character of heresy because of radicality. We will not only say that memory is 'owed' to the martyrs, that we owe them an infinite debt which we have not 'incurred', symbolized by a 'reparation' and a justice too often considered as if evaluable, or even by that hyperbolic reparation that is according to Levinas being-hostage, the substitution of the-one-for-the-other. But only a radical debt can honour the human-in-person in which everyone participates, and the Jews decisively as murdered.

## REVISIONISM 2: THE TRIBUNAL OF HISTORY

In general one feels that the tribulations of people, even of the Jews, without speaking for the heretics since it is not spoken of, falls within the tribunal of 'historian history' and sometimes, but more rarely, to philosophy and ethics. However, in the questions regarding genocide and extermination, of Jewish misfortune and the sufferings of heretics, we can only renounce any *supposedly sufficient* historical exegesis, including the notorious 'setting in historical perspective'. What is served by pushing historical studies to philosophy? The virtues of history are known – common objectivity, universality of comprehension, the establishment of a consensus where men can be recognizable, reconciliation with the past – but our problem remains this: is man a historical and philosophical being, as the *doxa* of intellectuals have it, and who calls for this self-knowledge and recognition? That very common opinion, the evident relevance of 'objective' and valid knowledge (supposing that it has that virtue by a dogmatic hypothesis), it is precisely this that puts blame on the victim. If we proclaim heresy in general and gnosis in part, it serves to immediately contest, by hypothesis, *the irrelevance in-the-last-identity of history for judging man*. We do not cease to carry the weight of the 'historical' and 'historian' nineteenth century, which the sinister twentieth has practically validated beyond every expectation. History appears in the World in an enlarged sense and can no longer fundamentally interest man as Future Subject. Of course the twenty-first century will make more history and will not make nearly as much of it compared to common 'culture', and from the calculations out of an equally common intelligence. But nothing of that for the generations to come who put themselves into what will not truly interest them. This is the same advantage for those disciplines levelling culture into a new common sense and they do not lay hands on a more essential point in man, on a *homo sum*, like a cogito, that they render more critical and necessary in forgetting and denying it. From the point of view that is human-in-the-last-identity history is no longer a criteria, not evidently of facts nor even of their signif-ication, but of that which is valuable for man, not as being-in-the-world but as he is subject-for-the-World.

Why is history, above all that of heretics, revisionist, in terms of its 'scientific' objectivity? 'Revisionist' does not here signify a falsification of facts, for example even the historian who acknowledges the entirety of the Shoah is a revisionist as a historian, since he implicitly believes to be able to inscribe in the universal element of objectivity, in time, space and that which they are allowed to mean, an event however in-the-last-identity. The human validity of history does not prove itself historically, by the historian's pretentions or hermeneutical considerations. A new thought, which no longer has the prejudices of history and humanism, radically fights revisionism. The anti-historicism is here theoretical, of course not practical, and it does not come to the aid of post-historical revisionism, to the contrary, but it wants to suggest that the latter makes a system with the perspective of all-history. The objectivity of these complexes formed by facts, their elaboration and their multiple interpretations are animated by a spontaneous tendency or a 'transcendent principle' to increase itself and to assert itself as absolute – *it is with this Principle of Sufficient History that every history becomes revisionist*. But for a transcendental science that is human in-the-last-identity, it is only a symptom of a new type. History must, like everything and following many ideals and conventions, lose its privileges, which are those of thought's conformism, and come back into the common order of knowledge or *doxa* out of which the World is made. It is in that condition that a really human science, through-and-through, finding perhaps less resistance ahead of itself, will be able to take it in its turn as a ground of experience. Heresy demands, more still than Judaism, that we call *'revisionist' every thought that believes misfortune has a sufficient cause and obeys a Principle of sufficient Reason or History*, that the victims come under history in full and are not, in various degrees, a-historical entities. This is the touchstone that decides between heresy or conformism and generalized revisionism.

In support of this revisionism, that is as dangerous as that of philosophy, another illusion speaks which certain philosophies are able to perceive. One of the great tricks of the Church used to discredit heretics and insure its rights against them is to regard them as de facto schismatics and not just as heretics. Every heresy is finally perceived as a form of schism or leading to schismatic consequences. The separation of fact and authority should appear less serious than that of dogma, but we conclude in general the latter from the former. Is heresy then one such separation of a part of the body from the Church? That is to retroactively assume that the Church-body has always existed, at least by right when it formed itself specifically in and by the struggle against that which, as one goes along that struggle and the victories won, has been declared 'heretical'. This is a kind of appearance from which the historians' 'explications' suffer, it seems that they always have need of a *telos*, will or end, in order to retroactively define the necessity of a genocide and to hasten it in spite of themselves. Some historians, for example, associate genocides and modern nation-states and assert, with a partial reason that they absolutize, the thesis of the will of modernity as criminogenic; they anticipate the existence of the criminal. In accordance with the logic of their auto-constitution, these states would feel their coherence of becoming-modern threatened by communities that by their own authority they started through ethnically and socially identifying them, either under the pretext of archaism or reluctance, by the seal of the stranger, which deserve extermination. The genocide would be a forcing motivated by the competition of states to participate in the acceleration of history, above all if the obstacle is interior, cultural or ethnic, as a long history [*un long passé*] and tradition which would paralyse from the interior the momentum towards modernity, and which it would be necessary to remove. But already this is an interpretation issued from a 'unilateral' point of view of awareness, perhaps that of the accusing victims, and thus also of the criminals who admit, internalizing it, this interpretation and who are condemned by a bad conscience. They do not see how the modern State, Church and their victims are tightly bound and themselves exasperate the one and the other in a battle without end. Genocides are fully justified coincidences where the anticipation of the criminal and the delay of the victim in reality form a system. However, it is not about drowning history in an all-genocide and a responsibility much too divided, nor about denying the suffering but only the possibility of founding a justice on it and the flattening which it cannot but carry out. The problem demands to be shifted. This is that oscillation of a point of view, that the other which is the complete reality of genocide, which is not unilateral in any sense whatsoever. Philosophy and history take the horrible empirical reality for the real and do not see that, however intolerable it may be, it is a symptom, the symptom of the hallucinatory foreclosure of Man-in-person via the convertibility of the criminal and the victim. The World is not a 'self-service' where each may choose whatever is convenient for them . . .

That argument retains a philosophical spirit but it deserves to be made the most of [*d'être exploité*]. If history is not the final judge of heresy and its destiny, it holds that it is not truly the original or first judge. Specified as that of the churches and carrying their constitutive prejudices, history has not *witnessed* the birth of heresies, it has not seen them be born because it is simultaneous with them in a system of anticipation/delay, it has been spun together, woven from that fibre that it has twisted and then tried to eliminate. Churches and heresies themselves co-belong at the origin, fighting themselves and the victorious forces, those which have defeated them, are the ones who have declared the others schismatic and voluntarily separated. The philosophical and scientific conception of history as meaning and as a discipline is compromised in and by that struggle to the death. Said otherwise, *there will be some (more than repressed, even foreclosed) heresy in the spiritual and scientific values of Christendom.* Their legitimacy is the contemptible right of the victor, the only right that in the eyes of the man who is only a man in not being one, or who is precisely only 'the-law' such that it constitutes itself in a unitary manner via power relations. The victors completely condemn the defeated (by all kinds of methods, occasionally gentle, of assimilation). But the defeated only condemn them in the-last-identity from the only radically human point of view that there is in them or inalienable to the anonymous forces of the World.

The gentleness and generosity of the victors is sometimes superior to that of the defeated, effectively threatened by resentment. But the problem of resentment is more complex than Nietzsche imagined it in the philosopher, he who, aggravating philosophy by inverting its privileges, defined the victim by the possession of conscience. Resentment is not just a 'metaphysical' interpretation of man, but a philosophical one, that which heresy rightly denies us. There is something more radical than resentment or its claimed absence. Man-in-Man is inaccessible to resentment because inaccessible to conscience, only the subject can in being affected by it and thereby being alienated. This is every victor's arrogant ideology, the superiority and right originally 'conquered' or 'acquired' in combat, expressed in philosophy and theology and all the way into the victims' mind. Heresy does not have the legitimacy of conscience, it only has the precarious right of the defeated. If it has a right *other than* . . . a legal one, it is in a justice that is human-in-the-last-identity. *Being a victim is without doubt not the sufficient condition for responding to the definition of man as heretic, but in the eyes of the World it is the necessary condition in order to manifest or testify to that 'essence', to that non-essence of man.* Every force, even victorious, is not criminal but every victorious force that considers that victory to be sufficient is criminal.


REVISIONISM 3: RESTORING JUSTICE, WHO ARE THE JUST?


Without doubt justice should not be left to individuals and their vengeance, but it must be taken away from the anonymous powers and dominations of the World which properly make or engineer 'individuals'. It can only be so in the proper or first name of Man-in-Man and its subject, the Future Christ. The victim is never unjust, it is even the Just-in-person, and the problem of the philosopher, the judge and the historian should be to make themselves adequate, with the specific ways that belong to them and that they must rework, to that unclaimed, and thus insufficient but necessary, justice. *The victim is a necessary but insufficient condition of justice in law and thought* and the fault of philosophy is to take advantage of that insufficiency of speech in order to simply substitute itself for it.

It is precisely in this that the victim is unthinkable, even as 'unthinkable' in the philosophical sense of the term, but requires a new experience of thought: a thinking *according-to-the-victim* and no longer *of* the victim. We don't ask the victim to think as the philosopher and the victim does not ask us to *think in his place* but to think differently in order to do justice to him. Does he even ask himself anything? In a sense and against all sense, he asks nothing and hesitates to manifest himself. But it is that particular science, outside of every silence-of-speech, that is the heaviest weight for everyone, a mute litmus test for a new way of speaking [*parole*]. The victim asks for nothing because demanding it, even justice, always risks assuming his misfortune is exchangeable and measurable with compensations of all kinds. It is impossible to invent a way of speaking, the beginning of a justice, that allows for the singularity of misfortunes and perhaps for more than their singularity – their identity? Instead of seizing the victim in representation's double evil, finding him in reality of little interest and making of him the lesson of objectivity and neutrality, the lesson of presence, it will be more just to consider his silence as the true neutrality that must follow thought. The victim does not follow a strategy of silence but can determine one on the basis of his secret. We believe in general that calamity cuts off speech and sinks into the unspeakable. In reality it suspends the old mythological and philosophical narratives and renews language by its Jewish interruption or even by its heretical determination in-the-last-identity. The Jewish calamity has not or not yet renewed their mysticism, only their ethics, while those of heretics found a mysticism of man without God and include an ethic of victims.

If it is so that every revision, even those resulting from good intentions, is a denial of the calamity, for example that of the Jews, *of which they alone are the measure, knowledge and memory*, we consider the philosophical problem of the Shoah as being here outside the limits of our project and subject by definition of the interminable mixture of opinions. We retain only this 'phenomenological' principle – suffering itself cannot be measured or compared one to the other always towards an end of revision and that this singularity, or rather this *identity*, is a reappraisal of the philosophical apparatus, of its inadequacy, and a firm demand to invent another one capable of righting crimes against human beings. The Shoah and perhaps more radically still, the continued murder of heretics without which there would be a contest in horror, are the sorts of ultimatums, addressed to culture and philosophy, of having to create another thinking which is no longer some simple cultural memory or hardworking good conscience. An ultimatum to conclude the war of philosophical opinions and, *though it goes without saying, as that purpose requires, but even for all that still requires we say it*, which will apparently not be followed up on if it is not understood, unless more profoundly it does not need to be understood to be followed. We have no threats to make nor arms to use apart from philosophical means that we solicit without enslaving. Concerning that ultimatum, the immanence of its being-performed is enough for it, its entire purpose is there.

It is thus not certain that we need to *restore* [*rendre*] justice as we restore reason (Principle of Sufficient Justice or surrendering [*reddition*] justice), and that the last word is *reparation*. There is no reparation for Man (but perhaps only for the subject) who is without equivalent or convertibility; this is no longer the reparation of the kind for the hostage, the substitution for Other people [*Autrui*] or *for-the-Other* (Levinas). This is the lesson of heretics, not of the Jews. *If it is necessary to restore reason to Reason, only the Man-in-person can give justice to the victims rather than 'restoring' it to them.* Heretics, and every victim witness to heresy, show us how to think up a radical donation of justice, not a surrendering [*reddition*]. If need be there is a restoring-without-surrender and it is Man, who determines every rendering of justice.

Who judges the exterminators, what legislator will be recognized as sufficient to judge the crimes against human beings? An international tribunal can be invested with the necessary authority to judge crimes against *historical humanity*, but for those crimes that are made against *human Identity* no tribunal can be constituted and recognized *a posteriori*. Who will establish judges for these crimes? *There are no super-just or legislators for this tribunal, the Just do not need to be established.* Who then are the Just? If they are not just by Justice in themselves or a transcendence that is within them (Plato), if they are no longer so by their act of reparation and their fate as a *hostage that demands an ever higher transcendence* (Levinas), if thus all philosophical and Jewish solutions are excluded in their principles, how will they be justified, by what event or what status? The Just are certainly not any positive and recognized historical human being, a 'metaphysical animal', nor is justice an attribute or essence. It is Man as a necessary but not sufficient condition of justification, a negative condition, either the justified or Christ subject, that is to say the ways of justice such as determined-in-the-last-identity. Once again it is pointless to appeal to a transcendent and exterior justification, under threat of falling into a vicious argument which would be that of the *Third Just.* If the Just cannot be so in themselves by the possession of the Idea of justice, neither can they be so in themselves as the hostage of the Other person [*Autrui*] *for* whom justice is, they are not just by an attributive relation or a religious relation but they are Justified-without-justification, without an operation intended to capitalize on the power of justice. Man-in-Man is that Just who determines every justification in-the-final-identity, not in developing all the pieces of justice – this is insufficient – but through their radical human identity determining practically the worldly ways of justice, including the victor's rights, which he dualyses.

The conflicting conceptions of justice – platonic by justice itself in the Just, Jewish by the Just as hostage of the Other person [*Autrui*] – are displaced and put into the ranks of justice's resources by a more elementary and non-metaphysical structure. That of unilateral duality from a necessary but insufficient primacy of the *last* Just (of-the-last-identity) over justice, and of a subject, *first* operator of justice and who in a way as first surrounds its negative cause. The Last Just (and not the last of the just) or the Just Cause does not create justice, that which is *for* the World and which must justify it, rather it uses the worldly resources of justice in order to 'clone' a subject justified-in-the-last-identity. The mechanism for justification is not divine or metaphysical, nor, in the interior of their mixture, does it distribute itself between faith and works. It is strictly human, immanent and transcendental and operates by a dualyses of the mixture of faith and work.

## MAN, CAUSE AND OBJECT OF
## PHILOSOPHICAL FORECLOSURE

Forgetting and repression, the holocaust and other crimes are without a doubt the human underside of the history of philosophy and theology. But these are not themselves only constituted on that underside and, for example, on a forgetting of Being and a persecution of the Other that they are willing to recognize if we are to force them here, but rather on an anti-heretical foreclosure deeper than a simple 'repression' or 'forgetting' and which, going beyond its recognized historical forms, presides over the birth and constitution of the dominant hallucinatory forms of thought. The logic of 'repression' is too weak to apply unchanged to the Greco-Occidental refusal of heresy. Why is the psychoanalytic and ontological paradigm (Heidegger) of repression and forgetting not more pertinent here? It presupposes that the last essence of things (the Unconscious and Being) are susceptible to being affected or even constituted by the repression and forgetting in general, that this ignorance or this forgetting to which this belongs by nature or force. And yet the One-in-person such as we have fashioned as the radical cause of every heresy, thus the Real, is by definition an 'unlearned' knowledge, initially foreclosed to thought but not at all repressed by it, this is not an awareness crushing in on itself, an unreflexive knowledge (it is neither reflexive nor unreflexive), or even an unconscious. It does not give rise to symptoms similar to analysis but only the language required to think it, but precisely because language does not determine it, and this is what distinguishes it from the great objects of contemporary thought. The One cannot be forgotten or repressed by occidental memory but hallucinated, giving rise to a special form of a symptom. Better still it is of itself outside memory-and-thought and determines them in that operation of foreclosure. Unlearned knowledge is not susceptible to forgetting and anamnesis, if it is not in philosophical language which serves to name it, but clones or 'produces' from the knowledge of phenomena of that kind. That which philosophy knows are almost unconscious and relatively repressed, the famous 'presuppositions', with which it occupies itself in returning to and what Judaism accuses and aggravates under the form of a repression or of an unconscious that it restores at the same time it is inadmissible and unimpeachable. Rather than a 'repression', Man-in-person is a being-foreclosed-without-foreclosure but determining it. It does not return or is not in control of an operation of recollection. It is entirely foreclosed to thought *because* by definition it never escaped man. Man-in-person is that *unforgettable foreclosure* that never returns, the *subject* distinguishes itself then from Man and becomes confused with the determination of the operations of forgetting and memory. For non-philosophy there is a truth to philosophy in having thought, whether badly thought or hallucinated, the One-in-person. Badly thought but necessarily well named since we have no other language than a philosophiable language.

Heresy thus makes possible a new thesis on man and the World. *Provided that one conceives him as Man-in-Man, man is un-forgettable and it is for that reason that the World attempts to forget him and believes itself able to forget him* by different processes, functions of philosophy and theology, ranging from hallucination to repression in passing through the transcendental appearance. Un-forgettable? Being in-Man and not in the World, it is given-without-donation, and the World is also given in-Man in the same manner but with a proper act of donation. Forgettable? That is the World qua one, although given-in-Man, can only, freed in itself, deny that being-given that removes its sufficiency. Man-in-Man is neither forgettable nor unforgettable in the sense of an opposed couple, but determining the forms of forgetting and memory that form the heretical-existant subject in its relationship to history. If there is a history of Being woven with forgetting and anamnesis as regards its own meaning there is nothing in it of Man and as a result there is a more profound history of Being and the World in their relation to Man outside-forgetting. Judaism has introduced into memory a fertile antinomy, unsolvable by philosophy but solvable by the heresy that attributes the unforgettable to Man and the forgettable to the World, distinguishing them by a unilateral duality without imposing on them a reconciliation in history or any dialectic in Being. How can we forget the radically Un-forgettable is the problem that heresy resolves or the contradiction that it dissolves in manifesting its philosophical appearance. Heresy is a lost past from before origins, outside memory rather than lost in the folds of history's unfaithful memory. Identical *in-the-last-identity* to its condemnation, heresy is a useless passion and gives rise to a thought unbound to any hope.

## NOTE

[1] I translate *existant* by "'existant"', rather than "'existing"', to express a difference similar to the difference in sense between "'dependant"' and "'dependent"'. So one is "'an existant"' rather than existent.

# CHAPTER FOUR
## Persecution and Revelation

PERSECUTION AND INDIVIDUATION

Between Heresy and Shoah there is a difference in kind more than one of degree or historical conjuncture. There is a reason to acknowledge an absolute right for the Shoah, since this is what it demands, but perhaps not a radical right, if this type of right still has reality here. There are two modes of individuation and determination, of human manifestation, which together distinguishes them from the pleasantries and terrors that form the standard Christianity of the church, the first by the immanence of Identity and the *cloning* that it enables, the second by the transcendence of the Other and the *memory* that it implicates. Under these two terms of radical Identity and absolute Other, of cloning and memory, we arrange that which gathers and distinguishes the Jewish experience and its equivalent for the heretic. Cloning does not at all exclude persecution but supposes another use and another mode of revelation for the human. Millions of people are otherwise and more profoundly expelled from our memory than those more recent 6 million Jews. Heretics have realized the fulfilment of that achievement *as* a second step into alterity.

The Jews have found a completely paradoxical identity in the absence of a reason to exist in persecution; without completely breaking it they have weakened the vicious circle of executioner and victim. Anti-Semitic persecution undoes the amphibology of the

Same but *undoes it without eliminating it a priori*. What is 'persecution' in this scenario? It is convertibility regardless of weakness or strength, of self and Other when it is hyperbolically twice compelled (the Other person [*Autrui*] is a 'higher other [*haut(re)*]' than myself, but I am more responsible for the Other person than he is for me because I am responsible for his responsibility in my eyes). The conditions for peace are identical to those of war apart from an absolute (irreversible) inversion and a hyperbole. The self exists as a sacrifice to the Other by the Other. The Jews have captured that which the Greeks ignored, reversibility's absolute blockage, the in-versibility of the Other or the relation-without-relation, in order to say anything about the affect of unilaterality, and they have passed on its heritage to us. However, this is a unilaterality of transcendence and risks seeing religion prevail over the human once again. Shall we be in our turn persecuted by the Jewish question? For if the Jews pass on to us a small part of the hell to which we have subjected them – and our new memory is that hell – then either we use that accepted culpability to raise the deeper question of the victim and of that which may be the world-man against the Man-in-Man, or we give in to the wild attitude of 'revision' and 'negation' to which they have given occasion despite themselves and because of us.

How does heresy position itself in relation to this limit-experience? More than absolutely repressed, heretics, as we have said about them, have been 'radically foreclosed', commensurate with their un-forgettable life, forgotten beyond every memory, worse than a supplement of alterity. Indeed, how can men kill men in the name of humanity? It is this paradox, formulated here in an all too general and ambiguous manner, that we must resolve and the ambiguity of the name of 'man' that we must dispel. The existant-Heretical-subjects have been murdered for their humanity(hallucinatory object) more than for their race(object of appearance and illusion), for their foreclosed being-human more than for an ideology of for the predicates of humanity, more exactly they have been exterminated by the World that anyhow exceeds these predicates and foreclose the human-of-the-last-identity. Heretics are precisely the human messengers against all-humanity and its 'values' of revisionism. Heretics have made 'the human' a name rather than an adjective, they have distinguished name and attribute, the first name and essence. They have performed the human name as the Real itself and have taken it away form the laws of the *Logos*.

Everything of memory and forgetting changes, then, as we have said, but everything of the Logos and the Real also changes. Rather than a new hyperbolicity, sometimes exacerbated and sometimes dialecticized, heretics have provided us with a completely other affect of the Real-as-identity, of the crime and victim and, in a way, have levied the sufficiency of the Jewish question by granting it the right of its demands. A radicality of the Real rather than of the Other which is always 'revisable' by Being, by its magical ability of denial. The radical past is not even intrigued by the present or conscience but transforms them into a new subject – the Future Christ. The heresy that cannot be formulated falls outside of that which can be formulated as much as that which cannot because it determines in-the-final-humanity another use of language.

What calls us to justice? The theories of exploitation and extermination (under all their possible forms) lead to concepts of the human that they want to be final: the proletariat, the plebs, the minority, the stranger, the Jew, the excluded, the resister, etc. All these theories are perhaps made in reality, without having taken the analysis far enough to understand it, from the finally philosophical point of view, which is to say from the point of view of the master, the powerful, the victorious, in general from the perspective of the owner of *theoretical* methods of production of which the philosopher and the theologian are the classic example. When summoned in this way they will demand to know by which right and by which offence. But in reality they have been called by the victim, by the exterminated all together and the long *theory of heretics* which develops *under* history. Thus, they will therefore reject this mixture, for them insane, and protest their difference. But it is not the victim who confuses them; they are mixed up in themselves and it is precisely their condemnation that comes from their being-mixed, which no longer tolerates Identity. These masters of the concept claim to define and outline the resister and the excluded, in effect they fashion it twice because every philosophical domination is divided and makes use of this division, it is the system of double domination. The revolutionary reversal of any hierarchy whatsoever in favour of the dominated term (so that is not insignificant in the history-world) is like a conclusion without premises since it has always the same premises, the dominating thought, and it lacks the 'premise' of the Real. Taking the victim's point of view – which is precisely not a contingent 'point of view' but a necessary condition, however insufficient, of any theory of justice – we assume the long series of concepts that designate the defeated of history as symptoms of a heretical subject.

## THE VICTIM AND COMPLICITY OF THE CRIME

Heresy does not know the 'memorially correct' or its contrary, without which it is a question of denying the watchful pitched against each other. Under whatever perspective that it is, as long as it is not that of scientific or ethical corruption and racist ulterior motives, we have never been interested in minimizing crime or suffering, in dissolving them in the always too vast geo- and historico-political 'considerations', to say nothing of philosophical generalizations like theodicy and ontodicy that challenge the subject's range of suffering and misfortune. Why an 'ideological victim', even 'whimpering races', a whole ethno-psycho-culture of peoples-in-lamentations? Happily enough there is Nietzschean laughter and the 'joyous-forces' which have already been included . . . As regards this 'dance', why is philosophy never as preoccupied with the dead as it is with itself? Why, despite the interest in bringing thought and justice together, does it not 'emphasize' [*d'« accuser »*] the right to suffering rather than the right to everyday recrimination, the right of the victim rather than everyone's same 'rights'? Raise the standard of thought and life from the position of their universality or justice?

If there is a right that we would voluntarily call 'absolute' but which could only be 'radical', it is that of the victim. The concept of absolute right is absurd and contradictory, but a right that is only radical means it is: 1. insufficient to contain analytically or synthetically, or in any other philosophical manner, the legal, ethical and material conditions of reparations (against the law of retribution, which reigns, from our point of view, in every philosophical reciprocity of crime and punishment, for example in reparation), 2. but it is necessary as the point of view unilaterally determining subjectivity's use and effects of the procedures of investigation and trial preparation, of punishment and the execution of punishment, which forms the complete system [*dispositif*] of crime and finally its complicity.

In one manner or another all the protagonists of a crime are implicated in or responsible for some part or aspect of the act, even the most passive victim, and precisely because he is passive-within-the-act, having there nothing in the World that can escape from the chains of responsibility. But not everyone is guilty of attempting to believe the spirit of confusion and opinion which, passing from responsibility to culpability, finishes absolving the responsibility on the path to the absolute limit and within that a change of order. The division between responsibility and culpability is each time determined, rather than created, by the constitutive unilateral duality of man. Culpability is said to be of the crime and of its agent in so far as they put forward, in a hallucinatory manner, Man-in-person within the 'victim' which has never been a part of the World. Undoubtedly crime immediately designates the victim according to the objectifying causality of the World, but it is the victim who describes the crime without 'calling' for this causality, but only determining it in-the-last-identity. The victim is only responsible as man in-a-world but determines in his turn the *identity of the crime* in-the-last-cause, the juridico-ethical machine that accompanies it. It is necessary to distinguish not just two notions, the responsible *participant* and the culpable *perpetrator*, but by adding that of the victim-as-determinate-cause who breaks the vicious circle of responsibility and causality. The confusion of responsibility, the concept of causality and everyday banality with culpability, as the concept of criminal causality that, in its most radical form, carries an ultra-worldy dimension, evidently serves to neutralize crime as a crime against human beings and *consequently* against Jews, heretics, etc.


CATEGORIES OF CRIME


Several major, overly confused concepts aggravate the problem of crime against human beings and prevent them from being clarified.

They are, as it were, 'philosophical obstacles' to the complicity of the crime:

1. The decisive distinction here is between the philosophical concept of totality or unity and that, heretically, of identity. The gregarious and unitary concept of *totalitarianism*, just like that of *generalized crime's* historical consistency coming to the support of a sterile conformism and revision, are self-encompassing of history. There is not a 'genocide' of heretics or of Man, these two concepts are as separate as the Heavens and the Earth, as biological life from the New Life. Genocides are historical, cultural, religious, ethnic, they are not universals as the invisible extermination is, the silent destruction of heretics from all sides. This crime is more than regional or fundamental, more than exemplary, it is as such the *identity of the crime* directly from the act set up against Humans. There is still less genocide 'of class' and 'of race' than they suggest. It is the only crime that addresses itself to Man-in-person and which demonstrates that it is at bottom an indivi-duality [*indivi-dualité*] and not just a world-subject, a position irreducible to the strength of the unconscious and which even calls for murder. The anti-heretical crime is transcendental and does not belong to 'totalitarianism', an apparently too narrow concept owing to the same confused generality, its empiricist extension and vague contours, a *unitary* concept almost unusable but, on the other hand, still indicative of a problem. Owing to its reduction to the identity of the thought-world, only operative because transcendental, 'totalitarianism' is a nest of amphibologies ('communism *and* Nazism') and contradictions, a great supplier of work for historians and intellectuals but little else. That a 'concept' as vague and also heavily burdened as this one can still be requisitioned for revisionist and depraved tasks, drives thought to despair.

It may seem insane to make, with a few nuances or precautions, totalitarianism a form of revisionism, and to set on that same plane those of purification, extermination, concentration, as if we had reformed one of these totalities. If we no longer believe in the supposed absolute value of these former distinctions of the plane (history and thought, crime and categories for thinking, etc.), if we still believe in distinctions as if properly 'absolute', just right to act in history and to add there (thus adding to the crime) but without real theoretical pertinence to explain it, it is because we rethink *each of these notions* in the interior of the practice of dualysis. There is at least one connection and convertibility in-the-last-identity, for example between ethnic purification and the theoretical purification of history. Inversely, one 're-writes' history *as if* one 're-racializes' or 're-ethnisizes' a people. Why should a claim to a 'metaphorical' use of notions pardon intellectuals and philosophers? Metaphorical regime or political regime? This is no longer what matters. Evil is not an object, region or a particular act divided from a more extensive set; it is a regime of thought, that the experience of the twentieth century has given us as a new task. If the philosophers of the last century felt themselves called or motivated by Greek or Jewish origins of thought, we feel ourselves called into a correspondence with the radical origins of ethics, which are not philosophical but heretical.

2.   What relevance is recognized, in the problematic of the crime against human beings, in *intellectual vigilance*? The use of opinion that philosophy makes, which it attributes to itself by nature, reaches its most equivocal point in the demand for a new right, the 'right of thought' or the intellectual's right, and among other things, to think badly and to protest against the excessive policing of 'good thinking' and 'speaking correctly'. These excesses participate in the control and generalized surveillance that comply with social life and can actually be overwhelmed by the kind of terror whose reign they spread over everyone and everywhere. But they do not always have the same signification and above all the same object, and the problem is that of the right use of the 'correction' of discourse. These mutual and crossed vigilances are intensified, with a supplementary degree, in the exchanges of the marketplace of ideas and discourses. They can only be exceeded by an elucidation, no longer circular, that, in this fight, cannot be an issue and only that which determines the use and harmony of vigilances in-the-last-identity. The victim is not an issue of vigilance, always moving forward anyway without any common measure with it, but that which qualifies and determines it as a new practice aimed at the crime as a complex object. We distinguish the generalized control of discourses and their incrimination-of-the-last-identity by the victim. It is no longer about thinking badly or thinking well but of thinking good and evil according-to-the-victim, this is the

only way to silently rid oneself, without the noise of opinion, of all conformisms. Heretical vigilance, for example, is better than forgetful memory, good conscience, resource and bad conscience of philosophers and theologians. The debates between historians and theologians about heresies, assuming them victims of the Church or venom poisoning the West, are interminable for reasons that go beyond them. How, except by identifying in the relationship of the West to 'its' heretics a foundational crime, does one get past these reasons?

3.    The concept of *identity* actually shelters the greatest equivocations. Ethnic, cultural or linguistic identification is the place of transcendental illusion par excellence and even of the hallucination as belief in the Real. It nourishes racist, ethnic, fascist and nationalist identifications. But it is also about identity as *unity*, identification or, worse yet, amalgam and blurring. And consequently only the real identity, that which is only found on its own human mode or which is its 'in-Own', can defeat unity and its criminalist and purificationist expressions. Only the Identity-in-person, and not difference, multiplicities or minorities, can defeat the depraved forms of identification.

4.    The *cult of memory* is a historical and cultural stereotype like the respect for the dead in an anthropological ritual. They cannot ground the reality of victims, but at most the ethical or religious postures that levels out man into unitary generalities. By what procedure is the reality of the man-as-victim assured? We must reverse and, especially, more than reverse the causality. It is the in-Man that qualifies and determines the act as victimizing. What respect for the dead, what memory could assure us that it is about men and not about simple bodies or waste carried by the flux of life-death? What is it that distinguishes a cart of carcasses from a cart of human cadavers? The mass grave of memory and a mass grave of human bodies? The essence of Man is not anthropological and it is not an essence at all, and memory is too weak, too engaged in the avatars of the World, for human Identity. It is memory that must be set in-past, if not in the past, and saved from its escheat and its doxic dissolution in the World for it to assure a new regime. Only the victims, because they are inalienable [*imprescriptibles*], can save memory, not the criminals. We can restore the right and memory, we do not 'correct' Man.

## AGAINST THE SACRIFICIAL IDEOLOGY

Let the hypothesis about religions, Christianity at the top, be as if founded on the victimizing sacrifice. The presumed innocent and the sacrifice that transforms him into a victim forms a system of convertibility that could give in effect the diameter of the religious sphere. The sacrifice can only have sense if it is of a pre-religious innocence which is not the apparent cause of its sacrifice. But innocence and sacrifice, more profoundly than any awareness can understand, are identical or the one draws itself towards the other in a widespread trail of bloodshed. This is precisely a crime and even the model of a 'pointless' or inexplicable crime – the original and prototypical crime that persists as anti-heretical crime. Through their divinity religions think of themselves auto-foundationally, refusing to be born or born from an ageless process. That hypothesis is also a typically mythological belief or a way of thinking. It cannot have any meaning and loses its arbitrariness if it is used as an experimental field for another thought and receives in turn an explanation. The sacrificial victimization explains nothing, it makes due with 'giving' in the vicious circle and in the specular operation of sacrifice which cancels itself out.

But how do we know that there are men and that they are victims if we are unable to learn it from sacrifice? Religion's complicity assumes through the victim another concept of the 'sacrificial victim'. In place of that pleonasm or this tautology, which religions place at their foundation, of this dogma which has the form of convertibility and the vicious circle, we place those axioms that assert Man who is in-Man, but not all men, as victim-in-the-last-identity. Non-Christianity says every man but does not say everything about them, and precisely it does not say everything of them because it speaks each of them.

## THE HUMAN AS POSTULATED BY THE CRIME

What signifies the Idea of a response or inaugural solution, still something other than first, if not that a new experience has been revealed with Gnostics and heretics and it may be the most radical human experience, from which the concept contains in a decisive way that of victim-being, but not sacrificial which is nothing else but a hallucination? If the extreme Jewish concept of man is that of the hostage and the persecuted, its universal heretical experience is that of a *being-hallucinable in-the-last-identity*. The heretic is perceived as existant so that precisely he does not *exist* as simply human and remains invisible. If he manifests himself, and he must manifest himself in order to be exterminated, then it is by his acts and beliefs, they are his relations to the World that express his invisibility in-the-last-identity or that witness to that strange 'essence' that is precisely being without-essence and without-existence, more generally without-consistency. Every crime engages with something other than a concept or a new mask of man. We postulate, for reasons of radicality, that heresy is the being-revealed of man in its non-consistency and lays bare its theo-metaphysical fetishes more radically than philosophical operations like 'doubt', the 'reduction' or scepticism.

Human being, in the Gnostic sense, at the heart of heresy, could well give a final notice to the old anthropology woven with the Greek prejudices and their ontological horizon. Regarding the *fundamental* question of Being, that animates the philosophical will to power and invests in theology, we substitute the problem of man as *determining-in-the-last-identity*, problem of his solitude and of what it can do. Regarding the metaphysical question of the *one* (being) who, because he cannot forget himself, forgets the *in* (one), the Gnostic problem of the *eon* the *in-one, of the identity and the subjectivity of man rather that of his being*. The problem of the defeated of history and the World are at the heart of the ontological affirmation of the strong and the dominant. Heretics are destined to be defeated, but the vital decision of the defeated has a completely different inclination than that of the victors.

THE HYPOTHESIS OF MURDERED MEN

Death, like birth, is reputedly absurd and unthinkable. But conforming to our problem the one and the other are neither thinkable nor unthinkable in the sense of that philosophical antinomy, but *thinkable as that which determines knowledge of life-death in-the-last-identity*. This theorem allows for a unitary confusion to be dissolved which renders impossible that knowledge and gives place to a philosophical pathos. Under these words, birth and death, philosophy in general confuses the Real of Man-in-person with the psycho-biological reality or phenomenon of birth and death in the World. Ontologically interpreted and idealized, these avatars of the becoming of the species are transformed in aporias. This is the idea of a unitary and anonymous *being*-in-the-world and of a *being*-towards-death, where it is always Being and Nothingness that reigns, imposing on birth and death a general and transcendent image. A life that is human-in-the-last-identity, that which philosophers have never been able to think, is incommensurable with a biological and social appearance and disappearance and even with a *being*-towards-death as a possibility of the impossibility of possibilities. How can Man be revealed, and revealed as a subject, by division and scission as is philosophy's way when he defines himself by Identity? It must be more than a 'repression', a foreclosing that itself has the form of Identity, it is crime and extermination that, on principle, 'gives no quarter' or will not be divided.

Let us take the case of death, which is more immediately apparent when it concerns the persecuted. In what more-than-tonal or more-than-affective experience does death reveal itself 'man', not in general – a unitary and thus aporetic concept – but man-as-subject (the Stranger), in what 'circumstances' does he die if not in that of his negation by the World as such? Death is not an ultimate possibility where the being of man realizes itself. Rather, it is the Man-in-person who *gives or makes death appear mundane as human in-the-last-identity and not only as biological*. Radical humanity, non-ontological, is *proven* when men are murdered and persecuted. The performation of their being-murdered and burned is in the manifestation and only persecution reveals as such the victim's irreducible non-consistency, only that non-consistency determines death as that of a human subject rather than of a 'beast'. Strictly speaking death reveals the Real less than it is not manifested by it. The onto-biological conception of life and death is a necessary amphibology but one that no longer returns justice to death as Persecution than to life as New Life. As there is a nothing-but-human life, a living experience extraneous to biological life, in some way the identity of a Living-without-life, there is a death extraneous to biological death and which only manifests itself phenomenally in an original experience, in some way a Dead-without-dying biologically or ontologically. This is not an attack on New Life, although that is a death proper to Man, it manifests itself as the resistance that is opposed to their subject. It cannot signify a destruction of the New Life, that would be an annihilation of the in-Man for which this type of problem does not present itself; it does not present itself except in the World and the onto-biological circle. From that point of view *onto-biological death is already defeated by Man-in-Man*. The prosecution of the World against the heretical Christ reveals the already-defeated-death and therefore the New Life from which we thus understand the irreducibility to the World. Not that the historical Christ's sacrifice had been the necessary condition for that victory. Human death can only be in-the-last-identity the effect of the hallucination brought about by the World of Man-in-person, with the constitutive repression of the subject. The very real murder of the heretic, his effective liquidation, is the effect of the hallucinatory will to destruction of the in-Man. It is in the anti-heretical crime that an immanent and radical death manifests itself, given in the human way of the Living-without-life. However it must distinguish between the 'already-dead', or the indifference (to the World) that appears in the New Life, and the crime-world, though seized by Life.

The problem must be extended to birth, examining it as much as death has been by the philosophers. If we are persecuted by the World as such, the persecution changes its meaning to agree with being born and also claiming to have the necessity of this being born. Unlike philosophy, heresy is a theory of birth as much as it is one concerning death. Human birth or existing under the sign of a persecution 'extends' to its identity. Therefore, do we understand, in the always unlearned manner, that we are irremediably doomed in birth as much as we are in death, in that contingency near to the World? That 'necessity' must be dualysed. In reality we do not know about mortals anymore than we do about immortals, if not by a biological knowledge that we share with the other animals. It is not from our birth or death that we are certain, it is from our being-human, it is from this that the announcements of our biological wanderings take their anxious character and acquire a capacity without a measure in common with those phenomena about which it speaks *in* the World. An experience more than affective and ontological, where it is Man-in-person who gives his power [*usage*] to life and to death. Man is not that unitary being who auto-asserts himself or creates himself as overman including his own death as 'last man'. We can only receive the contingency of death, from the events of the World, after we have received the contingency of life within the biological circle, but from the World *as such* we receive the persecution that makes life and death a symptom and assumes for them a human sense. We alone, regardless of our completely human insufficiency, our powerlessness in being born or dying, or rather because of it, transform the slaughter of men into killing as we alone transform our arrival on earth or our triumphant entry into the World and into a being-persecuted. Man was not designated from all eternity as a victim, a too general and contradictory formula, it is because he is in-the-last-identity a human that he is a 'victim of the World'.

Two deaths have thus been confused in 'the-death' as two lives have been in 'the-life' and their natural cycle. Death resulting from the mundane hallucination of Man-in-person has no possible forgiveness, and no longer any punishment, is without reciprocity or equivalence. The crime against human beings (rather than against humanity) puts an end to the onto-theo-biological aporias of the creature murdered by the creator and reciprocally the vicious circle of the victim doomed to vengeance. It is even more rigorous to maintain that, even if born, man defines himself as a victim rather than as a creature, it is in fact as a victim that he stops being an anthropoid in order to reveal himself as human. To onto-biological death and birth, marked by sufficiency, at once absolute and uncertain, we will oppose their reality as human in-the-last-identity which is 'radical' as they know the anti-heretical forces of normalization. The criminal is himself a human in-the-last-identity but allows himself to be blinded and enchanted by the World. It is not the criminal who is wanting, only the human in the victim in-criminates the criminal and convinces him of his hatred, not the hatred of humankind but of the human as such that he makes no -kind. This is the real content of the Giving of the Son and of his Crucifixion, putting the Future Christ to death, his persecution, revealing his radical being-human.

## LOGIC OF TWO PERSECUTIONS

If heretics are not simply repressed but denied as such and even as traces, then in what way are they persecuted? The methods concerning the persecution of the individual and social body, of putting it to death, suffering and contempt, are distinct; each type of persecution postulates a specific human reality and from there a practice of its knowledge. Within human cruelty and stupidity, there is room for all the churches and states, all the ethnic groups and institutions, and for their procedures. But certain distinctions are possible.

When they speak to the Other, and consequently in a privileged manner to the Jews, the persecution forms a vicious circle with a demand for alterity, there is an identity, certainly without confusion, of the victim and executioner *in a close but not absolute or hyperbolic inversion*. Levinas, for example, transferred to weakness all the characteristics of that strength which was exercised against it, from there a persecution of strength by weakness or of war by peace. In this way Judaism remains more than ever in the element of transcendence and alterity but absolute and no longer relative-absolute as it is in their Greek forms. There is evidently no reversibility between Greek and Jew, but an in-versibility or a unilaterality from which the Jew forms one body, to a close absolute alterity, with the Greek, the Other with the Same which it needs to fulfil the inversion. The anti-Semitic persecution is that relation of the Same to the Other that is not an ordinary inversion, with preparation and mediation, but a unilateral one without any preparations. Without preparations but not without an ultimate remnant of constitutive reciprocity since it finds it element in transcendence alone. Even hyperbolic alterity is an artefact that an overly simple awareness opposes to the Same and on which it grounds its existence.

That logic of persecution is profoundly transformed when the heretic takes over the Jewish stance, because then the One is strictly immanent (in-One) and not transcendent. At least in its principle or its cause heresy is not a demand for alterity, let alone for universal particularity (sect), but for the radical autonomy of human Identity. It is, as we have seen, the demand for an Identity that is more real than every singularity and every worldly universal (History, City, State, Being, Church) that is the spirit [*ressort*] of true unilateral duality. There is necessarily persecution because there is still alterity but an alterity without transcendence, the One-in-One takes responsibility [*s'assumant*] as *Other than* . . . immanent and affective for even the structure of the thought-world. But anti-Semitic persecution is in a dominant way a persecution in the World and in history and which exhausts its meaning, even the most transcendent, in history *regardless*. God has condemned himself to powerlessness and to non-intervention, to a vain attempt to intervene without being able to respond to it since he has chosen his people in history, even if it is a counter-history, leaving them to their despair and suffering, he is *bound* to them. On the other hand the heretic is without God and has not been chosen by a God, he is only chosen by crime and vengeance from which he draws out symptoms, only symptoms, of his 'humanity' and his alterity. Human beings are only chosen by their exploitation and prosecution which distinguishes them from Creation, those who spontaneously do not feel themselves either to be elected or damned as creatures would be, but only people-in-people, humans-in-multitudes.

There are thus two major kinds of persecution. One is 'absolute', it fashions itself against the Other that is itself absolute, which the persecutor identifies, persecuting absolutely but not without nuances ('race' . . .) – at the limit God persecuting God in his near particularity. The other is 'radical', it fashions itself about the Other as if in-One or as assumed by Man-in-person, which the persecutor cannot identify except by hallucination. He persecutes precisely because his attempts at identification are impossible and lacking reality, purely specular and thus ill-adapted. The persecution becomes anti-human and not only anti-Semitic when the passion of the Same for the Other abandons its transcendence, its deficient alterity and fades into the immanence of the World. Total rage and destruction, this then is what remains of persecution when the Other itself forgets itself in its immanence of in-One and disappears from the horizon of the World. In the face of that destructive rage without trace, the heretic can only put forward another rage, cold and without hallucination, completely defensive *a priori*. The paradox that drives the holocaust – making the Other exist as Other by his total destruction but maintaining him in existence by consuming him – is thus resolved, *there is no holo-caust, no 'wholly burnt', of heretics.*

## THE BURNED OUT AND BURNED UP

The heretic is more elusive than the unconscious accessible to anamnesis, or than the Jew accessible of the Law. The World itself symbolizes by fire its act of foreclosure. Fire consumes [*consomme*] or indeed engulfs [*consume*] itself without remaining, it is the performed par excellence which can only 'be done' with the heretic. One will object that the fire set upon the Jewish people does not allow heretics to be distinguished, if it is only the Jewish people who have been *burnt-out by a transcendent and technological fire* while the heretics are *burned up in an immanent fire without author*. In one case our living memory of being dead remains in ashes, of traces that bind us to the dead in our unbinding them. In the other there is a radical consummation, without trace in order 'to light' our memory. That without-remainder is the immanence of fire which 'remains' in itself, which 'immanes' as Man-in-Man. The light of the stake also has a right in its phenomenology . . . The *auto de fé* is the way that the World burns *itself*, abandoning a prodigious remainder, which is without traces. The *hetero-dafé* is the way that history and the God who backwardly inhabits it transforms the Jews into traces and ashes of memory. Finally, *the fire-of-the-last-identity*, universal and elusive, is for heretics and designates them as those who are only known in-Man. Without counting the rationalist and atheist in-cineration, the return to an immanence-of-dust, which completes the perfection of the World, its transcendental constitution as Hell.

Why fire, which wants nothing, instead of simple nothing? Fire is the Other against the Other, it is the great revelator of the Stranger and the phenomenological counter-act that manifests him in a destructive light. It is an operation of simulation and or a mimetic of alterity in general, of the Stranger as inassimilable. It puts an end to the delays in the process of reappropriating what is not negotiable. Out of this fire, which nourishes them but which they also fear, philosophy has only captured and phenomenology only retained the flash and the glance [*foudre*], then the sparkle of the phenomena or the brilliance of Being, then the light of the Good thrower of shadows, finally the dull, small rational light that Nietzsche endeavoured to re-kindle. This is why history as the history of philosophy is a history of fire and begins rightly with Greek and Hereclitian fire, with which it traces the first and definitive figure of the World, philosophy illuminates itself as a self-portrait. The glance is used to assess self-assessment in the World that it outlines. It is an identity of immanence and transcendence, a machine at once hot, cold and overheating. Philosophy as search for the absolute is not at first sight a crematorium like certain religions or racist ideologies, rather it will be nuclear in its origin.

This system of fire has been divided on one hand in the experience of a fire of incendiary transcendence that attempts to exceed itself, a hyperbolic fire destined for the Jews, and on the other hand in the experience of the stake which has more a fire of immanence destined for the heretics. Burning up is an act more radical than absolute, but the absolute *consumes* and *therefore* cannot consume everything of the empirical, cannot go without traces, while the really inconsumable, the heretic, is *engulfed* and leaves no trace as it demands hallucination. There are several kinds of victims. We *use* fire or gas, it is a technology, against the hardliners of transcendence like the Jews, we torch their life and language, as though this fire has effects which complete it (suffocation) and allows a cadaverized memory of bodies and history to remain. Burning out the Jews has been a true culture . . . But more simply we burn up the heretics, who are of immanence, that of in general, knowing science, mysticism, even philosophy and theology, we burn them in the name of their knowledge rather than in the name of their 'race', because of their spirituality rather than their 'biology', 'history' or 'economy'. Burning out is economic in every possible sense and often in the appalling sense when it is about the Jews, a sense which is not completely exhausted in the logic of sacrifice, that of the Same to the Other and consequently of the Other to the Other. The destruction of heresy is addressed to alterity only second, and first to Identity. In the anti-heretical crime, there is nothing to understand, no logic in a revolving door of argument and motives, except for a pure vicious circle, no dominant – or even illusory or false – argument (race, conspiracy), but a hallucination in front of which no 'explanation' can be received that is capable of making sense – like talking to inquisitors. Heresy does not merely interrupt the economic logic of exchange and non-exchange, it does not restrict equivalence, gift and sacrifice – the heretic neither returns to the Other nor does he sacrifice the Other, without the risk of retaining a remainder of reversibility. It determines in-the-last-humanity that economy.

## JEWISH ALTERITY, HERETICAL ALTERITY

Ir-reversibility is not an autonomous concept but, as a relation of syntax, it needs a real support, either the Same and Being as an empirical base which is possible to reverse – this is Judaism; or the One and Man-in-Man determining in-the-last-identity – this is heresy. Either the repeated or absolutized Other, or the Other-without-otherness or immanent because given in-Identity. Heresy does not make of the Other an absolute or an infinity but frees him by the radical immanence of that absolution. The Other that Judaism has revealed as absolute, heresy has revealed as radical in subordinating him to that which is no longer a principle but a completely positive an-archy or unconscious. *An-archy* is an ambiguous term and can be understood, in the manner of an adverb, like *Otherwise than* essence, or even understood in a still less ambiguous way combining the proper name and the adverb like *Other-than...,* as Without-essence. Who is the least anonymous, the most dignified of the first names, God or Man? In Levinas, as a limit-example, who moreover finds in Spinoza still too much of immanence, we find still too much of transcendence. It is obvious that only the Real is irreversible. But either the Real can complete itself in the Other and takes the form either of a height or an absolute withdrawal (the infinite distance of the Other as One also), or first from an absolute also designated by relativity (Heidegger, the retreat of the One as Other also). Otherwise it is the Other who can also exchange itself for the One-in-One but without repeating it, as being-separated by immanence or *Other-than . . .* In these two philosophical cases unilaterality receives an essence that consists in an operation of absolute inversion, without return

FUTURE CHRIST

(Levinas) or of a half-real, half-ideal 'turn' (Heidegger). The thinking of Being and Judaism coalesce their efforts (in deconstruction) to endow the old philosophical transcendence with a Real under the form of an absolute transcending but more or less still hobbled in ideality and essence. It is another affect of reality, the Real-without-transcendence, that heresy teaches as untaught. The slogan of twentieth-century thought goes *from the Other of Being to Otherwise than Being* and it is this problematic that heresy uproots as horizon of thought without any claim to destroying it. Neither Levinas nor Heidegger freed themselves from the vicious circle of the World from which, via diverse operations, they perpetuated the humanly fruitless conflict. Only the heretics use the Greeks without being Greek in thought, and the Jews without being Jews in affect.

THE FINAL RESISTER

Our categories, like those of genocide or holocaust, are inadequate for thinking the criminal grounds that in a way accompany the final civilizing role of history. A humancide rather than genocides, a crime expressing Man-in-Man rather than the kind, species and their individuals, this is the *telos* of the final-identity that the churches and states pursue without wanting it, wanting only minor crimes that allow them to survive. The updating of crimes and tyrannies, their growing visibility, the vigilance of the intellectuals and the counter-controls of institutions created for that end, not directly showing that which are only symptoms and devices of substitution – a universal foreclosing of Man-without-figure or unconscious. The Jews are a privileged victim, they expose history but are not that which we have called the Last Victim, that which returns history, ethics and religion themselves to their place under the Law of the World.

Of course, there is no beyond of Judaism, the Last Identity is something else. It is about defining *the last possible resister, the heretic, who draws his strength precisely from not being beyond* but in-Man. Because the last resister is necessarily the victim and not he who is opposed to domination, he is the exterminated and he is the burned up, he is not

110

that sub-victor, that marginal or minority with which recent philosophy, which has not changed and is always that of the powerful and victorious, wants to exchange itself. It is necessary to acquire the theoretical methods of understanding that in-the-last-resistance is Man-in-Man, the radical defeated, from which history, its defeats and graveyards, only suggest symptoms. It is that only the defeated practically transform history and make use of the victor himself. The Jews are still not that final resister, only the Baptist who announced him but who announces nothing but the inversion of philosophy, Christianity or simply history, without trying to reappropriate and realize itself. The Jews have nevertheless ceded to us and we have received from then, in one way or another, an infinite debt, but heresy is a radical debt such that it does not receive itself from other men or God, as every man gives it without having received it and only produces it. This is why the heretical point of view allows the vindication of the Jews in a spirit of appreciation and not benevolence, in gratitude and not condescension as that of their integration or assimilation, their reinsertion into the State (Hegel) or into the Economy (Marx).

Philosophy knows a *final, as much as initial, solution*, it is 'supersession' [*dépassement*], which feeds the worst fantasies.[1] We call 'heretical' precisely the defeated resistant to supersession himself because only he can practically transform it. It becomes impossible to generalize the servitude in all-mastery (the identity of all-mastery and all-slavery), as philosophy does, and to sink into the confusion of the victim with the dominated adversary or the defeated enemy. The adversary of the victim also changes shape. Taking that of the 'World', gathering together domination, exploitation, extermination, concentration, purification and even other provisionally more beneficial effects, it ceases to be the hydra or leviathan external to the philosophers, its being-manifested makes it take on a double function. Finally, it appears as that which concentrates the strength of foreclosing opposed to Man-in-person, and as the simple occasion and material of the heretical subject.

We expect from heresy, perceived at first as a fact without thinking or like a protest historically or religiously trivial, a renewal of thought, no longer according to an alleged new ideal, a meditation on Being or on the Good, on the One or the Absolute, but on that ultimate ground of history perceived from a distance by Judaism but where the heretics entered. *Evil remains for the Jews a promised Earth, that where the heretics are buried for good.* The Jews exceed the history in which they appear and in which they have left traces, heretics refuse history and set it in heaven because they still place man elsewhere than in heaven, that is, nowhere or in-Man.

The Jews are only an event of history and of memory insofar as it inscribes them there at an inopportune moment [*à contretemps*] and assembles them in this strange manner, the heretics transform them in expressly giving them the identity that they do not have.

### NOTE

[1] I have followed Ben Brewster's translation of *dépassement* as 'supersession' in the English translation of Louis Althusser's *For Marx*. *Dépassement* was one French translation of the Hegelian *Aufhebung* popular among French Marxist-humanists, and I have used Brewster's translation in part because of the influence of Althusser on Laruelle's work and because supersession is a term used in discussions of the relationship of Christianity and Judaism in theology.

# CHAPTER FIVE
## The Last Prophet or Man-Messiah

Human beings have a problem that only they can solve: what to do with the World? Salvation or rebellion? Exploitation or therapeutic? Consumption or consummation? And, as those variously premature responses to that question, what use can be made of Christianity, the churches and gnosis? Modern philosophy has not hesitated to propose its own style of salvation to Christianity and to God himself in restoring him to the essence of man from which he would be alienated. One imagines the infernal laughter of God when the dialectic stands him on his head announcing a philosophical salvation . . . But we who do not believe in the dialectic anymore than we do in Christianity and who no longer practise them only out of boredom or a lack of anything better to do, or even out of conformism, what salvation are we able to offer God? What gift can be made without resentment to the creator and passive spectator to so many of our misfortunes? He did not witness the creation of the World and its redemption, a creed which limits Christianity, he *is complicit with and has his hand in the World* as gnosis denounces him, and does not cease to compromise himself with a creation living as a failure. And it is of little importance whether it is a failure or not; it is the symptom that is important which we force to incriminate it.

What an error in ever having said the 'essence of Christianity' . . . Man is without essence and he removes the essence of Christianity more so than Christ removed the sins of the World. Definitely ambivalent and a madness-without-rigour, Christianity *tears itself down* and only tears itself away from and then returns to the World. Definitely particular, gnosis *entrenches itself* in the World, dooming it in its loss and locking itself in a solitude of sufficiency. Definitely desperate, sterilely *mixing* Christianity and gnosis, philosophy only makes the World complicated and reinforces it. How, with the Christian ascension which removes itself *in full view* [*à la vue*] of the World but with 'saving' it *in mind* [*en vue*], and with its Gnostic *rejection*, can construct a treatment that is no longer of the World by the World close to God, but of the World by man close to Man? How, without reconciling them in a system, to conciliate these two postures into a unique 'assistance for the World'? How to invent for the World, with these conditions that we inherited, a human-and-only-human salvation? What salvation is still nevertheless possible for God and his works-crimes? What renewal [*recommencement*] for his failed creation, his complicit silence? Do Christians too know what they do? And who forgives them if they do not know? Our principle of precaution is this, a theoretical caution regarding faith – we neither know as a believer nor as a philosopher that which we make when we 'believe'. But we can begin to think that non-knowledge and ask *what to do with Christianity rather than what makes a Christian*? This is the problem of a 'non-Christian' repetition of Christianity and in particular of gnosis.

## WHAT IS TO BE DONE WITH CHRISTIANITY?

Let 'the-Christianity' be the writing of that mixture that we know, in its infinite tensions between faith, dogma, temporal and spiritual authority, who yet hope to confess an ecumenical faith from a common origin – unitary aggregate validated by common sense, history, and finally theology and philosophy brought together. That writing testifies here to a unity in question [*en cause*] but that we take in its pretention as a symptom for a future decision. 'The-Christianity' is too simple a notion and must be explained and finally transformed in a 'non-Christianity', its true 'non-Pauline' universality.

Now take it that what we believe to know in 'the-Christianity' by faith and intelligence, by prayer and dogma, inwardly and outwardly, have been set between parentheses. We withdraw our faith in faith, we dualyse that philosophical doubling, we renounce and give up the former in order to better acquire the non-believer's understanding of faith. For there is one faith that we will call operative, more profound and more ineradicable than 'religious' faith, a faith in faith that makes possible and exacerbates its self-defence against its suspension and even sometimes against the proclaimed faith and its dogmas.

Finally take it that we ask, in knowing that it is sill possible to make something with 'the-Christianity', what future use of it is still allowed to these heretics whom we call humans? We renounce the demonstrations of faith, history and philosophy, in whatever apologetics there are concerning the truth or untruth about a Christianity assumed 'true' and 'in itself', from which naively we search for its essence or from which we prognosticate the decline or the renewal, the 'end' and the 'return'. Our problem is one of use, and so to speak practical, but according to a new experience of man, precisely non-Christian, such that it allows without contradiction that suspension.

Now, who is this 'we' who suspend their faith and refuse to give into faith? It is certainly not planetary or worldly philosophers, those who do not wonder what to make of the World-in-person. It is the 'we' of the Future Christ, the Christ-subject who we are without having by hope or obedience indentified ourselves as such, identifying that we are already in every way as Man-in-Man, subjects merged with their non-Christian performance. The theory of the Future Christ is the immanent practise of its theory; our only faith is practical and additionally a pragmatic of the old Christianity.


## WE, THE WITHOUT-RELIGION

The conjuncture of non-Christianity is not that of the 'end of Christianity'. What one conceives of on the model of an 'end of philosophy' declining in itself, exhausting its last possibility, incapable of inventing itself or even of developing itself in new dogmas, or that this end is its dilution in the World and its opinion, in a vague idea about 'religions' and their conflict, none of this, which is still real to various degrees, sufficiently leads to the undertaking of a Final Good News. At the very most that conjuncture is occasion, material, signal or indeed even simply a motive, of the Future Christ's birth, but certainly not the cause that makes it necessary. Moreover, do Christians know that religions are also mortal? It is of little importance if Christianity is eradicated from the surface of the Earth that it stretches out across. The hypothesis of its radical contingency, that of its replacement does not affect the principle but only the programme of non-Christianity, also contingent on its occasion but based on its cause which makes it necessary in the time of Christianity from the start as at the end. In order to announce this Future Christ it is necessary to be without religion, but not having lost it or even protecting it within the conformist forms, for this is not a lack of faith or an excess of empty religiosity that this would entail, of a decline of churches or a resurgence of sects. That is only an occasional cause, as we said, and assumes another necessity, just no longer only for that simple occasion. Non-Christianity moreover cannot claim to enter into history and change it, and maybe it will sink with Christianity or will not even have the time to be born. *Nevertheless, thinking it is already to practise it.*

That cause determines the announcing of the Future Christ, necessary but insufficient since it needs these occasions, it is the being-foreclosed of Man to religion and faith. Removing religion in God, it removes God and Christ from religion as well from the churches and from the devices of the church designed to subjugate human beings in calling them to build it as subjects-of-faith. The Man-in-person is an a-religious being but only he can become religious or come to faith, because everything conspires to bring it about that he bears the World's mythologies as soon as he becomes subject *for* the World. The indifferentism in terms of religion is a historical fluctuation that affects human beings but, we will see, has nothing to do with the indifference that is the essence, or rather the non-essence, which makes them real. This religious non-consistency can finally explain their fury in giving their faith over to the World's 'paganism' and the history that feeds religions and their apparatuses.

Devoid of religious consistency, human beings can nevertheless 'with full knowledge of the facts', that is, without reason but not without occasion, devote themselves to a practise of religions that being an adequate usage for the humans they are in-the-last-identity. Religion without dogmas, but in axioms and variable theorems according to their object, the ancient doctrine, the old-new testament. With the cloning of every man as *subject*, humans, despite or because of their in-sufficiency, take up existing under the form of an *organon*, precisely the Future Christ, the authentic relationship to the World and to history in totality rather than in the manner of their phenomena. The old Christ had been conceived in transcendence and the World (in sin?), he was without doubt an organon but still on the model of mediation or instrument (for a reaction or a rebirth). Christianity cannot overcome its failing of identity and faith by a profusion of churches and orders, of dogmas and authorities, saints and priests, actions and ritual operations. The Future Christ rather signifies that each man is a Christian-organon, that is to say, of course, the Messiah, but simple and unique once each time. This is a minimal Christianity. We the Without-religion, the Without-church, the heretics of the future, we are, each-and-everyone, a Christ or Messiah.

The Last Gospel is thus not a programme designed once for all, in the end persecuting. By its final cause, it is without end, without teleology. By its practise, this is only a half-programme, only unilateral, of a constitution of the Christ-subject giving aid to the World and against it. The most human heresy is future and practical by its essence in-the-last-identity, theoretical and pragmatic in its ways.

## CHRISTIAN AND HERETICAL

How do we conceive a heretical repetition? In order to be resolved, the problem of the Future Christ calls for new distinctions that are no longer made in the interior or exterior of Christianity but at the same time with it, with its help or occasion, and *to the radical exterior* of it in a manner paradoxically immanent and heteronymous. These distinctions take the place of the old problem in its essence. There is in any case, we have said, a causality by immanence or radical identity that takes the place of the problem of its onto-theo-logical foundation. Concerning the Christ-subject, he calls for transformations which are profound, but which follow from this last causality. We are given as material the Christ and *also* the Anti-Christ, that we are careful not to forget. We substitute for them *the non-theological non-dialectical duality of the Christ-world and the Future Christ intended, by its construction, to destroy the sufficiency of the system of Christian theology.* To practise non-Christianity with the help of Christianity, in order to undo the narrowness and the prejudices of that last system as religion-world, this is not deconstruction and its theology with it, once again carrying out its 'criticism' or finally freeing the 'true Christianity'; it is determining in-the-last-identity or in using it under a human regime, a regime barely humanist . . . And it is consuming that which can be it, not 'the-World' in general – not more pertinent than 'the-Christianity' in general – but its authority, the-World-as-domination-of-dominations.

But between the Christ-world and the Future Christ who is for the World there must be found another source capable of taking Christianity to the power of non-Christianity without constituting it as a simple variant – it is the figure of the inadmissible heresy understood as gnosis. Faith and knowledge . . . heresies are only such because they are Christian, we tell ourselves, deviations or oppositions to a dogma. But we believe that heresy, above all under its Gnostic form, contains very few Greek and Christian pre-suppositions about man and is sufficiently deep to be inaccessible to any theology. This is why future Christianity announces fusion-without-mixture, identity-without-synthesis of Christianity and heresy – we maintain the duality of the historical denominations as religious postures given in history. Incommensurable postures and so all the more susceptible to a non-Christian mixture or one without-mixing. So the figure emerges of a Christ as Great Heretical Subject, a subject that the 'son of man' could have been but that he has not been. A 'Last Good News', as it were, or an ultimatum.

## THE LAST GOOD NEWS

Non-Christianity is universal because it is about the human Identity of an end other than salvation [*à l'autre de salut*] and not about God, decidedly too particular and too partial. Man is a mechanism of salvation in three states. The first is his state of only finding himself or identifying himself in-Man. This is less a first state than a primacy over the World, the refusal to begin or not begin 'Greek' or even 'Jew'. The second is the state of man-in-the-World, wherein he is interpellated by Christianity and some other dominations who constitute him as subject-in-hope. But this is the second, for there has not been a first state. The third is the true first state, the state-of-priority of man over the World and it is in that posture that he emerges as Future Christ.

There is no 'end of time' (or its modes, end of metaphysics, end of history, etc.) in the diverse sense where common sense, helping philosophy, can understand it, so this is not like having penetrated philosophy with a religious or mythological imaginary. An assumed end of time does not outline the theoretical space of a new messianism, of a renewal of faith. Future Christianity is not justified by a philosophical conception of time, but by the human reality where it finds the necessary cause for use, a use of that experience of time and history. That experience occasionally serves to name the three instances of a time-without-temporality which is neither ecstatic as the radical past as 'Time-in-person' is, the present as World or Whole of time, finally the future as Christ-subject. The cause of time is the Living indivi-dual [*indivi-duel*] but not as factual possibility or even efficacy, the heretic is no more a phenomenologist than a metaphysician. Time is immanent to time and not to anything else, it is the in-Time, abysmal and barren, a character who would belong to mythology if he was of this World. It is thus a radical past, this is its form as cause in-the-last-identity of time-subject's temporalization. The heretic is not acquainted with phenomenological distance, transcendence spread out in *meta* or tightened in *epekeina*. The One-time is an unlearned knowledge or one without consciousness, unteachable by a historical or supra-historical experience. At the 'end of time' which was only announced with time as temporalized and temporalization, we oppose the Future as an undivided emergence of the time-World's clone. This time-subject is, by one of his sides, in-past and outside-world and, by his other extremity, a use of the time-world. This is the principle of a non-theochronology such that it supports the announcement of the Future Christ.

It is in this framework that the Last Good News inscribes itself. If the ordinary 'Good News' is the ecstatic announcement of *ta eschata*, of the last things, those which ring in the end of time and gather them together in a Christo-logic parouisa, the Last Good News does not ecstatically announce transcendent events trusting in the time of expectation, it only announces itself, it is performation but without auto-annunciation. If non-Christianity was auto-kerygmatic or even hetero-kerygmatic, it will continue to understand kerygma as an announcement deferred in various ways and will not be Future Christ 'in-person' or 'in-practise'. This is why the only announcement is the same practise and does not have exterior content like a messiah to-come ahead of our hopes. The Final Future rather than the last things, in ecstatic expectation which waits for nothing but its practise. The 'final identity', in-Man or in-Past, does not prophesy about itself and for that reason it makes a Good News possible after which there is no longer anything announcable. Last because it is practical. The Future is the identity of the first and the last word, at the turn of centuries as at the start and end of time, it is the Prophet-in-person, the Messiah.

## THE FUTURE AS ULTIMATUM

Our repetition of Christianity is not itself Christian, no more than that of gnosis is Gnostic. Can we 'possibilize' faith and religion like we do with philosophy, promising without giving or else interminable donation and mediation? A knowing practise rather than one believing in faith, such is *the good news because final*. We practise a special messianism, of the ultimate and the minimal, sobering up faith – simple material – and of course theological sufficiency. The possibility is the last possibility or it is only a lie. We no longer hope for the order of the finished event or an infinite messianic expectation. The Messiah-subject is a stranger to the waiting-for-the-Messiah like the Christ-subject is to the return of Christ. If we still expect a possibility, it is not the richest and the most promising, the parousia of the final judgement, but the last possibility and the poorest.

Our proclamation of a Future Christ is a performative kerygma, it is not a promise or a message still indecipherably carried in humanity, it is an *ultimatum*. Either peace is an ultimatum or it is only the expectation of a war and perhaps a war of expectation. Man is that *Ultimated* who determines Christ as an ultimatum and instructs thought to have an in-the-last-identity in order to carry assistance to the World. The churches and sects, the large and small dominations have jointly secured the re-appropriation of the living by putting them, and their constitution as hopeful subjects, on hold by their insertion into time and *in* the World. Defer and rule… Christianity is all set to supply a sufficient Reason for faith, albeit a challenge to reason, but non-Christianity is from a universality of the Real rather than from Reason. How then will the Final Good News not be an Ultimatum, made by Man to philosophy and theology, of having to help the World and not only to care about being in its entirety and the cause of being?

We have only an unlearned knowledge or only a gnosis, it is of the radical past, only a rage, against the present, only a faith, it is the Future. To practise the Future from the present or in its intention and occasion? To announce the Good News and spread hope, or to perform it against all hope? If we announce nothing on the order of a message, it is because *our expectation is something other than our practise* of Christ rather than his 'imitation'. Our kerygma is an act and performation, it is a Promised-without-promise and which the promise does not defer. A promise *in-real-time*. We practise the Future Christ rather than that waiting for the return of Christ, just as we practise the Future rather than announce and imagine it, we perform it as the last possibility, that which was not in reserve but which was the 'in-reserve' itself, as the most irreducible messianism according-to-the-past. A promise in-real-time is a promise *according to* real time, that which *was* on the mode of the 'in-reserve'. And real time, that which has never been and could never be announced, but which *has (been)* lived and performed, this is Man-in-Man. One philosophy has strongly maintained that time was the Concept, another that it was Being, why would it not be Man? And as for the radical Future from which it is provided that title, as the eternally messianic dimension of the in-Past, why would it not be the Son of Man in the face of a non-Christ? The Final possible prophet, in other words than the first, is it he who holds himself in the in-Past and who does not stop announcing the Final News and making an ultimatum? 'Future', always being an adjective, gives us in itself a first name to designate man as liable to being-cloned. As much as the Self, the Subject, the Other, the Stranger, etc., the Future must acquire the primacy and dignity of a first name intended for the human. This ultimatum? Man-Messiah exists . . .

## HOW DOES CHRIST COME?

Without thereby reducing it, the Christo-logical experience begins with the historic Christ but involves a refoundation of time and history as historicity of the transcendental kind in general beyond empirical time. That new temporality is structured like that of a doublet, first and second coming of Christ. From the one to other, the unity of time is understood either as expectation of a resolutive event, the presence in-parousia of the Messiah, or in a less metaphysical way as a strained awakening to the imminence of that coming (Heidegger, for example). But the desert mystics who mimic Christ's return and the thinkers of unique imminence still have in common thinking Christ's coming as *split in two*. The old form of return, from an ontic future time or from a content that makes a representation out of faith and an implicit contract out of the promise, that waiting there continues to live in humanity's fantasies. For the less metaphysical thinkers have interiorized the expectation as awakening, tension and imminence, as structure of care and facticity of life in its relation to self. Heidegger has put the self-comprehension of life-as-time to work, possibility as structure of comportment to self and temporality, rather than the efficacy of life in time, phenomenological distance as tight and 'mine' rather than slack and scattered in spatialized time. Time has become principle of all individuation in being an unmasterable possibility of *Dasein*. However the novelty of that harmony of time is in fact limited in history and has only been carried in the interior of philosophy. The transcendence in *epekeina*, that which is a pure opening almost without end or closure, interiorizes that in *meta* and tightens the philosophical Decision on itself, transforming it in possibility. This is a realization of philosophy that does not abolish its sufficiency, as if Heidegger made use of Christian faith and mysticism without giving them anything, for an eschatology simply less deliberate than that of believers.

What really brings about this simple weakening in the general structure of metaphysics and its double transcendence? Whether it is event and advent, reconciliation of Christ with man or a strained conciliation, it is always a double coming or 'accomplishment' more or less interiorized. The historico-historial doublet is *structured as* a metaphysics, displaced and dug up, but it does not invalidate it. In order to resolve that vicious aporia of splitting, we have distinguished the time-cause, given and living without the help of the World, from a radical past which has nothing to do with an immobile eternity; the time-mixed of temporality and temporalization, which is equivalent to the 'enlarged' present of the World; finally the time-subject which 'starts' as cloned from the second by the first. This is time such that it is the living-of-the-final-identity of the 'simple' who do not wait for the return of Christ in order to have time but who know that everything is finished and that they have the task, which is completely different, of producing Christ as Future time. The in-past is not temporalized, only the time of the subject is constituted from a double source, worldly time and One-time which clones the subject-time. Cloned time, neither pure past nor transcendence 'in-memory', is the Future as ecstasy non-ecstatic (of) self. Returned to its principles heresy extracts the past, the present and the future in every historico-worldly eschatology.

Heretical time, a human identity of time, thus avoids this solvent splitting and that philosophical necessity of being that which could only be called too justly a 'recollection' or a retreat from time. The Future Christ does not come *in time* as its historical and religious figure neither does he *return* as its messianic figure, deploying the time-expectation as awakening to a presence. The Future Christ is time as subject-time, cloned or born but without a birth brought about in the time of the World. Christ comes thus for the World as the identity of a *Future-in-person* who has never been divided by history. *Ta eschata*, the future things are no longer merely anonymous things or events that would be deprived of the authority of the Logos, but subjects that emerge by immanence and the solitude of Hell's mixtures. They do not have to repeat and realize an ancient promise, to mimic and imitate the historical Christ with a view to bring about the return to earth of the operations of a hermeneutic magic of auto-comprehension or mystical gestuality. Why imitate Christ when it is Christ who, in his being-cloned, imitates Man? In inventing with these ways, which are the ways of the World, but always with the Time-without-memory of the radical Past, Christ is.

## THEOREM OF HUMAN ASSISTANCE

We call 'human assistance' the relation of struggle with the World but having in mind the carrying of assistance to man in the World and thus to both of them. We could have maybe said 'humanitarian assistance', but it would then be necessary to first 'save' the 'humanitarian' from its global politico-humanist sufficiency, elaborating a theoretical, but certainly not practical, anti-humanitarianism. We already know that it is not about founding a self-defence of man against the World and which could give them their last meaning in the diverse kinds of struggle (class, faith, subversion and revolt, etc.). The great question which drives ethical philosophy when it does not lose itself in the clouds of Good and Evil and then catches sight of its ultimate object in man is *who must protect who and how so?* Philosophy is divided as always by a contradictory response and falls into an *antithesis of protection and assistance*. Its first maxim says that the weak must be protected against the strong, the second that the strong must be protected against the weak (Nietzsche). There is a labyrinth of the strong and the weak where philosophers get lost. The problems begin with these terms which need completed, the weak protected by the strong or by the weak? The strong protected by the weak or by the strong? Philosophy thinks it leaves that labyrinth in gathering them together in a unique, speculative formula: *strength is the strength of the weak and the strong*. It is and means *the auto-protection of the weak and the strong, as they mean their auto-domination*.

The decision between Kant and Nietzsche does not matter, since it is according to Reason, sufficient reason for protection, finite or infinite. The problem is not of protection or defence but of knowing if they are, as philosophy believes it to be, auto-protection, auto-defence, or if the protection of this victim is 'human-in-the-last-identity'. The solution requires no transcendent cause but expresses itself nevertheless by the *a priori* rules of a new style, by a certain 'logic' of practical formation and production of our acts and designed to break, by unilaterality, the vicious circle of opposing auto-protection of the strong and the weak. Therefore we substitute for the poisoned problematic, around which philosophy revolves, the human problematic of man's defence by man such that it is no longer just a vicious circle. We expound a transcendental theorem that must determine each time according to the conjuncture of form and above all the sense of struggle as protection of the subject as in-Man whom no loner needs an auto-protection. *Man-without-defence, without consistency of the strong or the weak, and the defence of man-in-the-World as subject (in the occurrence as Christ-subject) are identical-in-the-last-identity.* As devoid of strength and weakness, Man determines necessarily, though in a insufficient manner, that defence for which he needs the means-of-force offered by the World but that he precisely reduces to the state of means by precise operation, in particular by cloning. We will call 'human assistance', in order to contrast with, among other things, 'humanitarian' assistance, with its political, humanist and ethical motifs taken from the World, the effect or the contents of this theorem as it has Man for a cause, the Christ-subject for an organon, and finally man-in-the-world, its sufficiency, hallucination and its transcendental illusions for an object. Only the philosophical ideology of strength and the agonistic can believe that this is about a timid and timorous thought in a state of auto-defence and not a universal human theorem.

# CHAPTER SIX
## Toward Non-Christian Science

MODELLING CHRISTIANITY RATHER
THAN GROUNDING IT

'The-Christianity' and 'the-gnosis' are unitary formations, mixtures and between-memberships for which we can despair of finding a method of theoretical examination that renders them intelligible. In other disciplines such objects are labelled 'complex'. What method should be followed in order to master this complexity of data without twice denying it, first by an objectification without thought and second by a philosophical and conceptual idealization? How to enter there from the outside (without repeating that hermeneutically), but by respecting its specificity (with reducing it in a positive way)? Entering from the outside into Christianity, in these original objects of faith and dogma, with the joint help of science and philosophy, is a theoretical challenge of a new type but from which the conditions escape from philosophy's sufficiency as much as from the positivity of science, but not at all from those disciplines *if they are partnered according to a fixed relationship*. We will call 'modelling' the construction, by the unification-without-synthesis of these two disciplines, of a unified-theoretical representation of Christian faith but also for it. Refusing to look for its essence and to idealize it, to dissolve it in philosophy, completely refusing such a reduction of the positivist and materialist kind to other phenomena, we maintain its relative autonomy at the same time as its intelligibility by the means of *this type of scientific (and) philosophical representation but without mixture which is the model, such that it can be adequate to these kinds of objects.* A model of Christianity rather than its essence, its theoretical repres- entation rather than its concept, its reality rather than its theoreticist and dialectical dissolution in the alienation of essence, this is the task of modelling and it is something other than a structure, always too ideal and relational. For objects of a philosophical type, the model is the combination of an *a priori* relation of the philosophical or tran- scendental *type* and a relation of the scientific type to the experience to model. These two original postures, irreducible the one to the other, form a strange set, the 'model', on the possibility of which it must be examined but which provides the intelligence *for* faith. The old combination of faith and philosophical reason in a sufficient 'intelligence of faith' is too short and must be more than extended, complexified in a now non-Christian intelligence of that faith. Thus that intelligence is to double the theoretical means but, in the Real, it is under the unique transcendental condition of a new species called 'determinate-in-the-last-identity'.

Having thus avoided a philosophical-idealist deviation and a scientistic deviation within the method, what material is utilized for this operation, what exactly models so that we don't fall into another deviation, this time 'Christianist', that comes from an excess of Christianity's presence alone in the object? 'The-gnosis' may be that way of universalizing 'the-Christianity' from the point of view of the experience to model. 'Faith and knowledge', this is the formula of a classic problem of modern philosophy and also the indication of a symptom that has not ceased to shape the constitution of Christian dogma and its authority. Re-activate the heretical posture in its challenging of every worldly authority, revive its long and burning struggle with the Church and its hatred of heresy, combine them in a unified posture of faith and knowledge of salvation, this does more than intensify Christianity, it carries it to the *non*-Christian universal- ity that applies to every man beyond his religion and confessional background. Separated from their philosophical and Gnostic husk of dogmas and images, faith and knowledge must become identical but, of course, in-the-last-identity rather than in a synthesis, in a new and hollow religious system.

## DETERMINING THE MODEL IN-THE-LAST-IDENTITY

What is to be done with Christianity? That question, we have said, goes to the conditions of its radical or non-believing intelligence, by a modelling evidently adapted to the specificity of the 'human sciences' and philosophical but used also, in this case, by the heretical principle of gnosis. However, the pursuit of these conditions cannot focus on this stage, under threat of asserting 'transcendentals' but, in the manner of philosophy, idealist and theoreticist ones. They must be acquired inside of a radical setting between parenthesis of every philosophical sufficiency of faith and Gnostic knowledge, lest their materiality will be destroyed. A possible operation if a real-transcendental condition (in a new sense) determines that non-Christian and non-Gnostic modelling. We know its first names, Man-in-Man, vision-in-One, Living-without-life; it remains to reformulate also in its turn, according to that material in order to rigorously proceed, which is to say by respecting the specificity of our object without reducing it to other phenomena or other 'vocabularies', for example sociological or unilaterally Gnostic, and leads to 'deviations' that are in reality philosophical normalizations.

Of course, it cannot only be about an axiomatic formulation, of a play of decisions and linguistic designations that do not decide on the Real or do not name it in the philosophical way by pretending there to make it come about in its essence. The concrete non-philosophical work implements the entities of thought-language, of ontological or theological 'abstractions' and produces from them new 'abstractions' that do not belong to the Real but to knowledge in its own reality, which thus modifies our relationship to the World in rendering it adequate to Man-in-person. For example, the vision-in-One is axiomatically asserted by an act of *premiere ultimation* that asserts it as an 'ultimatum' *for* Christianity. The axioms can describe it, along with all the contents of the non-Christian model, with the help of immanence, of life, separation, faith, the world, salvation, etc., and of the most immediately theological and Gnostic categories, but submitting them each time to an appropriate work of abstraction.

We re-formulate in this way and in these limits, with the help of the Gnostic 'vocabulary', some effects of Man-in-Man. He is the determinate cause in-the-last-identity of salvations or of the non-Christian subject because he is inalienable in religion or under the form of a divine projection of his essence. Poorer than nothingness itself from where it has been created, he refutes the decisive character of God, Creation and Redemption in the definition of its claimed essence, because he does not have essence or existence, the one or the other or the two together. If Life is already short of worldly consistency of being in-Christ, what about the human living-without-life? Because he only finds the human in him and he finds the World also in that way, he is without theo-gnostic essence in general, without anthropological consistency and, for that reason, may determine a non-Christianity without being in its turn determined by Christianity, a non-Gnosticism without being convertible with Gnosticism. The Real is foreclosed to essence and the language that supports it. This is to reprocess the theological terms according-to-the-Real and not according to faith or the understanding of the human sciences.

The symptom is Unity-*in*-Christ on which the churches are based, on the mode of Expectation, of a radical immanence that is that of the *in*-Man. Waiting-in-Christ is the hallucination that creates the religious foreclosure of Man such as it responds to the being-foreclosed of Man to God. Unity of the living is not equivalent to the universality of Identity that protects the human from religious alienation. Even the immanence that can be assumed in the auto-generative life of God as *causa sui* or as infinite auto-affection of self is definitively less from creation than from the sacrifice of the Son for the World and his empty tomb. The creation of humanity and its redemption, the necessity of a divine plan and providence sullies God with a transcendence that does not deny the attributes of his perfection and his being, *on the contrary*, as it sullies humanity with the insecurity of its creatural transcendence. The religious crime is a parallel situation that resolutely exposes man in the World and alienates him there; it exceeds the simple original error and cannot be made the object of a redemption of the kind of that of man. Because God himself can no longer make sacrifice in order to save himself and man with him from that situation and that sufficiency, then we wonder if the crime is not due to an irresponsibility that would have reinforced the irresponsibility of the onto-theo-logians. No new cross is still possible, no Christ is once again situated towards Calvary and it is necessary to invent another salvation for God-the-World himself. The Unredeemed-in-person will be the cause and will be able this time to rescue God from his evil vocation, and from the curse with which gnosis has rightly condemned him.

Vision-in-One, this is not the 'most high' principle but most radical, by its *immanent identity*, as Unity-in-Christ and, by its *being-separated-without-separation*, as Gnostic separation. Man as if shed of Expectation, of faith-in-Unity. As if he was the living experience of a Christ-in-Christ who, still more than its model, would overcome death. The Life of the philosophers still lacks immanence as it has not become the Living-without-life and is not separated without having received the separation that takes away the view of the World and removes the World from its view. In its greatest immanence philosophy remains suspended in Life's transcendence in self, in its auto-generation and auto-production and is never sufficiently separated nor ever sufficiently oriented in the World, doomed in its salvation in as much as it is not of this World. A non-Christian heresy is possible when it is the immanence of the living which of itself is separated from life. If the historical Christ gave life, the Christ-in-Christ is the subject that nothing or no one has given and who has no need of salvation but who can give it to the World and to the God-of-the-World.

Finally, we distinguish:

1. Man-in-Man as the Real or as vision-in-One, the Unredeemed who determines-in-the-last-identity a non-Christian and non-Gnostic treatment of Christianity,
2. the Christian postures (the Expectation of the unity-in-Christ) and Gnostic postures (unilateral Separation) as methods of modelling or procedures of the treatment of world-Christianity,
3. the *non-Christian heresy* as resulting from the modelling of Christianity and the determination of the model by the in-Man. That determination will in general be understood as the cloning of a non-Christian subject from the World. As the Son of Man, strictly speaking.

## NON-CHRISTIAN MODELLING

We take it as given, because we have exercised it elsewhere under the name of 'unified theory', the principle of the modelling of experience, via the duality-without-mixture, of the philosophical or transcendental posture and the posture of scientific objectivity. For it to be completed, this modelling must still combine, in a duality equally without-mixture or an identity-of-the-last-instance, the two minimal and invariant postures of faith and knowledge. An overly brief phenomenology provisionally discovers there a phenomenal content of which the generality does not make an obstacle, to the contrary, of their essential heterogeneity that prohibits or denounces their historical mixtures. The Christian faith is *faith-which-unites*, Gnostic knowledge is *knowing-which-separates*, two ways without any comparison but they both intend to assure a non-worldly salvation.

In this modelling, the World seems to be object and means of salvation at the same time. Non-philosophy is a theory of the World in the most universal sense of these words. It extends the concept of the World beyond its cosmological and theological significations, prolonging them and amplifying them from philosophy ('the-philosophy'). So there it includes 'the-Christianity' and 'the-gnosis' that traditionally conflict there, but which in reality only oppose a restricted concept of the World, limited by their well-known Greek presuppositions. That amplification is only justified by a reason proper to non-philosophy, that of the Real as One-in-One (Man-in-Man), cause-of-the-last-identity who decided on the World not only as Being and Thinking but as enclosing every possible experience that involves one form of transcendence or another. So has that thought-world become for us a system of axioms and does it not exhaust itself in an intuitive definition of the object ('the-World'), always intra philosophical and in the process of being overtaken by the same fact that belongs to 'the-philosophy'. So although the thought-world must be redefined without ceasing, in the limits of its system of invariance and variance, according to the experiences to be modelled. But as this is there the only exploitable data also with the aim of obtaining the objects as well their rules, we must draw from the World the data to treat, which are, at the same time, those procedures of that treatment. This is why we make use of these two titles, 'the-Christianity', reduced to its minimal posture of faith, and 'the-gnosis' reduced to its posture of knowing and separation. These two terms evidently have to be rearticulated but we provisionally assert them as first terms necessary to advance knowledge and to construct a 'non-Christian' model of Christianity. In a general manner, via a demand for coherence and in order to respond to the cause-of-the-last-identity, we make use of Christian faith and heretical separation as procedures of salvation, which is to say a unified treatment of the authority and the sufficiency of the World which in other respects belongs under the given form of their mixture between them and with the World. We make of their new non-philosophical combination an *organon* of determination for ultimate salvation.

That treatment of the World, not by the world but by Man in-the-last-identity, is a transformation that is a salvation. Two phases which are identical but without confusion form them, a unilateral duality of necessary phases in order to fulfil them. This is, on the one hand, the construction of the model itself, construction of 'non-Christian heresy', and on the other hand, the determination-in-the-last-identity of that model by Man-in-person. Constructing there a model of Christianity, including gnosis, is their true 'deconstructive' intelligence because that is their full human-and-only-human usage against the spirit of subjection in the World. Strongly prompting Christianity to a unilateral decision about a heresy, taking away from gnosis its dualism of mythological imagery . . . But giving to heresy the power of transformation from a faith, taking away Christianity's old spirit of conformist domination. Non-Christian heresy is a supra- and even non-historical hypothesis of fusion in-the-last-identity of faith-which-unites and knowing-which-separates. It is intended to definitely remain such a hypothesis and to keep its universal strength of heresy. Bringing Christianity back to Man-in-Man, thus without reducing it to a humanist essence, it liberates *the heretical as subject and the Christian as heretical* from Christian violence as from Gnostic narrowness.

It perhaps seems possible to reduce the material and the procedure to only gnosis without embracing triumphant Christianity. But this would be 'Gnosticism', like we have said of 'theoreticism' (which is not theory but its Greek exclusivity) or of 'Christianicism'. The exclusivity of gnosis contains its own danger which is that of a refusal of other religions that is itself religious and a conception of a new sufficiency of unilaterality. There is a Gnostic Heaven-world that makes a mirror with the Christian God-world as soon as gnosis is treated like a unitary entity and assumed self-including, as a new idealization and when it is not reduced to the structures of its *philosophiability* by right, preliminary reduction without which the use of non-philosophical categories and devices have no sense. Passing directly from religious gnosis to non-religious gnosis means reaching the Gnostic theory without simultaneously struggling against the philosophy that is in it, without taking into account the *philosophiability* of experience which confirms the pretention to the absolute validity of religion in general and gnosis in particular. Only fundamentally religious minds can postulate that religion and gnosis are autonomous as self-including. It is important to distinguish heretical unilaterality, of making a good use of it, and a 'unilateral' heresy that in its own religious sufficiency delights in itself. This is why an experience that is not abstractly unilateral but a source of universal unilaterality must be sought as capable of identifying-in-the-last-identity faith and knowledge and so of determining them as procedures for a new salvation.

## COMPLEXITY: TO STRUGGLE ON TWO FRONTS

Modelling Christianity is to take into account its nature as a complex object, sects included here as an example. What serves the sects and more generally mythological and religious madness that are more or less mastered and organized? It causes vicious and linear explanations, either idealist or materialist, but always a reproduction of the thing's state to explain and to do so in a unique sense (reaction to 'materialism', evangelical fermentation, mask of political exploitation, renewal of community solidarities, globalization and loss of the local, religious moralization of the market's inherent democracy, globalization or to the contrary the fragmentation of society, etc.). The 'human' disciplines want to resolve, above all, the problems of genesis or of productive and genetic causality instead of limiting themselves to a determinate causality of a material of knowledge (as the sects are) that is given and received beforehand. Hence their bad unilaterality, misplaced towards the inadequate spot, in the World, their linearity and their understanding of unilaterality as exclusion. These logics are regional, though sometimes fundamental but still regional by another turn of thought, content themselves with adding to the World without explaining it.

From the point of view of the object to be made intelligible, each of their reasons is acceptable since it is not exclusive of others and since it is considered as co-belonging to the philosophizable complexity of the phenomenon. Even the old religious obscurantism and social underdevelopment are true reasons along with fear of death, the worry of inserting religion into the new technological environment or of preserving it, of reforming society, etc. From the point of view of method as well, it is necessary to struggle on two fronts, abandoning thought by a *circular* unity-cause, fighting the unicity of the historico-worldly cause, even 'systematic', and substituting for it the identity-cause that is neither unity nor system. Fight the linearity and substitute for it the determination-in-the-last-identity. These vicious causalities backfire as means of exploiting the human subject. This is why to explain is to struggle, making intelligible is to undo the exploitation not of Man but of the subject, transcendental hallucination and illusion from which it is the object and which indirectly commands the forms of its exploitation in the World. All religions have means of exploitation – they are necessary to hold them together – but not in the intellectualist and Voltairian sense of the Enlightenment. Not only the sects, as we reiterate, but religions in general, have always been a problem of public security, an interior and exterior enemy. But if the sects are conquerors, reformists and revolutionaries, and practise a *fully justified and acceptable* exploitation in name of all possible ideals (against communism, against the states and established churches, against Complicity [*Intelligence*], by fundamentalism, by ultra liberalism, for the 'Western Christian', in the name of the past or even the to come [*avenir*], in order to acquire the dignity of reason, etc.), the 'grand religions' and the churches coming from sects are completed by handling the acquired situation and often, though not always, contribute to the general stabilization, which makes them preferred even by secular States. But moreover the completely relative softening of the struggle *in* the World and the struggle against and for the World itself are two different things of which only heresy decides in determining a new modelling of these phenomena.

## FAITH AND KNOWLEDGE: FROM PHILOSOPHY
## TO NON-PHILOSOPHY

'Faith and Knowledge' is an ancient topos of the relations of gnosis and Christianity according to the intervention, explicit or not, of philosophy as a third term, a common ground re-activated by those philosophers talking about 'German Idealism'. We have already extricated the minimal contents of faith and knowledge (in the Gnostic, not scientific, sense) as 'postures' rather than as 'principles' of Christianity and gnosis. For that we have variously suspended their ontic and ontological, and of course historical and dogmatic, determinations. Without engaging in comparative phenomenologies of these unitary formations that are not our object, some precision is called for because it is with that duality of postures that a model of Christianity may be constructed.

Faith and knowledge are ambiguous terms, above all when they are taken up again by philosophy and mixed in doctrinal combinations impregnated by metaphysics. In the absence of a more precise description, we will put it in a manner already bolder and more complex: *Unity and Separation, both unifying and both separating.* The Donation of unity, donation by that which is already unifying Unity, and the Separation of unity – here Gnostic knowledge – thereby even in its unifying turn, are invariant schema, susceptible to infinite variations. Whether they are explicitly or not philosophized, they are woven anyway into philosophy, incomprehensible without it and moreover always philosophizable, threatening sufficiency or the absolute, the form-world. In the historico-religious efficacy the two 'principles' are mixed and measured according to various proportions under the authority and rule of 'the-philosophy'.

On the other hand it must already posses the unlearned knowing of Man-in-Man in order to make that which we have made here and there, extracting from their mixtures these specific postures and *delivering them from their auto-positional and sufficient conception.* For example, the attempts to distinguish faith and philosophy via their objects or their representations are artificial and superficial since that history is itself busy combining and mixing them. These distinctions are made on the ground of that mixture and are thus still an expression of it. We wrongly suppose that the mixture of two thoughts can be the veiled and presupposed means of distinguishing them, still that philosophy will itself make a speciality of these vicious circles. Their distinction by the kind of thought, or else of method, is apparently more pertinent, for example faith as an ontic object of this science that will be theology, and the fundamental thinking or auto-understanding of Being which will be what is peculiar to philosophy. But the difference of the ontical and the ontological, of science and philosophy, is still here an internal difference in philosophy as a comprehensive structure that implies the inseparable and finally convertible mixture of these orders, mixture of terms *assumed* pure and autonomous.

Why is this mixture carried out in history? It is that the mixture philosophically dominating ('the-philosophy') philosophy and science, and the mixture religiously dominating ('the-faith') philosophy and faith accompanies by its contents, having a fundamental operator in common, transcendence that combines an element of ecstasy in *meta*, an element of ecstasy in *epekeina*, and finally an element of objective or noetic and noematic content from representation. In short, a complex transcendence, itself repeated thematically and operatively. We may generalize that structure as 'phenomenological distance' in order to oppose it to immanence, and in order to understand it also as 'faith'. But it is there, in fact, a reduction that is completely insufficient and simplifying because transcendence operates in the background subsisting in that reduction. Measured then by the radical immanence of knowledge from which the Gnostics have given us the Idea, unlearned or unteachable knowing, thought and faith reveal a transcendence that is truly universal and which we will rather call non-decisional or non-positional (of) self. That transcendence non-positional (of) self is a residual transcendental matter, not a common or unifying element, but specifically each time as postures of thought and faith.

The slogan 'faith and knowledge' receives significance now by symbolizing the non-philosophical duality of the philosophico-religious (faith) complex and that which it is opposed, the heretical identity (knowledge). We make a double use of the Gnostic theme of 'knowledge'. On the one hand as unlearned, real 'substance' of Man-in-person, on the other hand as procedure of salvation confronted in faith with a view to modelling Christianity in the enlarged sense which we mean. If rather we distinguish radically on the one hand, rather than inside philosophy, under the form of a unilateral duality, knowledge determines-in-the-last-identity the philosophico-religious faith, cloning from the former a new form of faith, and relatively as they are two procedures of salvation forming here a duality of a mix and no longer a mixture.

## THE IDEA OF UNIVERSAL NON-RELIGION

We call 'non-religion' in general every theory that is unified, not spontaneously but in-the-last-identity, of a religion or confession with philosophy. As we have seen in the case of Christianity, this kind of theory, universal by its cause, has an interest in universalizing that religion, also from the point of view of material, by the means of another principle or by bordering ones, for example Gnostic ones. It is about destroying its particularism, the exclusivism of its believers, its fanaticism, reaching that which we do not dare to call a 'ecumenicalism-in-the-last-identity' (more so than in the first authority as Church and with some philosophers, like Leibniz), making from the church's authority a new use and freeing human beings from their religious servitude. In effect, we cannot universalize in a non-philosophical mode except by a cause-of-the-final-identity. This guards itself from believing that the extension, the synthetic multiplication of material-religions is sufficient for achieving that universality. Non-Christianity is not a religious syncretism, rather it is a radicalization of the identity of a religion that is from now on not exclusive. These religions-subjects or these Christs-subjects themselves opposed in every way to the authoritarian and anti-schismatic integration as to the debility of inter-religious 'dialogue'. Inversely in order to reach a universality which does not preserve the illusion of sufficiency proper to a religion or a confession, we will avoid attaching ourselves to a single particular doctrine, like 'the-gnosis', in order to balance the Roman Catholic doctrine, for example, both turn to mental and doctrinal imagery. It is impossible for non-philosophy not to work with these massive doctrines, it is a universal theory not *of* the axiomatic *kind* but making use of the axiomatization and which takes for its objects those already constituted bodies of knowledge called 'intuitive'. Still it must limit the illusions of sufficiency bound to solitude and doctrinal exclusivism. 'Faith and knowledge', Christianity and heresy, these are the minimal dualities that we can agree to without falling into syncretism.

## FROM THE PRINCIPLE OF SUFFICIENT FAITH TO THE NON-CHRISTIAN FAITH

The modelling of Christianity is the material content of the Christ-subject which is, for his part, his being-determined-in-the-last-identity, that which we call his clone. We go back over these procedures and their becoming as Christ-subject. One of these two procedures utilized in that end is Christian faith, the other being Gnostic separation.

Faith is, without a doubt, a decision on one hand; it also possess an aspect of transcending and projecting. But this is not an empty transcending not even in the nothing. It is a decision of faith rather than of theoretical knowledge, of practise or ontological projection of a horizon that will auto-affect itself and be divided. It is not division first and turning onto itself. Foremost it unites but without horizon, return or withdrawal, or only uniting in-Christ. Uniting-in-Christ is at once its object, its end and its means of union. That uniting is a donation of Life and only gives Life in uniting the living in that manner. It thus also separates itself but only separates from the World in uniting via the Life-in-Christ, which determines the separation. Yet, it is an immanence of the in-faith rather than an immanence of the in-Real of in-Man. There is an order of phenomena, the separation is ordered by the unity of Life, this by the unity-in-Christ, and this by the donation of that unity. All the rest may even be theology and philosophy, at best phenomenology. That generality is enough for us, our end is not to establish a 'philosophy of Christianity', not even a phenomenology of the donation of the Life-in-Christ by sufficient and absolute recourse to philosophy and faith, a recourse that is forbidden to us, but to describe faith as a procedure of a possible treatment of the World with the goal of modelling 'the-Christianity'.

If non-Christianity must fend off a pretention, it would be that which makes of faith a principle and gives it an assumed real value, less faith itself to transform in a simple procedure than its sufficiency in the measure where it tends *to justify itself* and cause a Principle of Sufficient Faith. In spite of its donation by grace and history united in Christ, or because it is still the object of a donation, faith contains a final ecstatic ingredient, as an auto-affecting expectation with which it joins a call to account for man as subject. It is not empty but possesses an object not of scientific or even Gnostic knowledge, but just of expectation. Thus it does not expect Christ as an object in time or history but as the Life-in-Christ. Its expectation is the phenomenal content of *the immanence of the imminence* of Life. Christian phenomenology is not Greek and philosophical; it flattens one on the expectations of the other, time and life in a positive phenomenon of immanence.

But if Christians wait for Christ inside of expectation, the last identity of the Expectation and Christ under the form of the Future Christ is still not acquired in this way. Time and expectation, transcending and decision, even if they are auto-affecting, they are precisely only auto-affectively made, remaining partially outside of themselves. They may always, for their part, be seized again by phenomenology. Even to admit that faith is not a simple mode of originary transcendence, a mode of Being or 'phenomenological distance', that it is more immanent or even more transcendent than them, the Expectation remains an affected immanence on its back and in its origin, either by the empty tomb of Christ, still transcendent, or by a transcendent call, and this suffices to hand it over to philosophy. Inversely it is not necessary to have a 'philosophy of Christianity' in order to see that the latter may also affect the former. This is why faith such as we ascribe to the Future Christ is a posture extracted from Christianity as a material but must, in our vocabulary, be determined or cloned as human-in-the-final-identity or 'non-Christian'.

As Heidegger has formalized the question, and as Kant began to do so in order to make belief rational, it is necessary in effect to formalize faith, not only to analyse it in its multiple kinds (religious, specifically Christian, rational and philosophical), but to dualyse it from the point of view of its transcendence between those forms of philosophico-religious obedience and its non-Christian form. We have gathered these religious and rational forms in a minimal invariant, ecstatico-vertical transcendence (*meta* and *epekeina*) such that philosophy can show it despite the nuances of its object, rational or religious (a temporality between expectation and hope in Christ). But the essential phenomenon necessarily escapes the presuppositions of every philosophical and theological analysis and remains invisible in the most living and most originary faith, always unitary. It is that 'the-faith', without repeating itself or dividing itself into two species, is *dualysable* and not only *philosophizable*. Dualysing means extracting and manifesting the ultimate identity of faith that 'the-philosophy' and 'the-theology' do not think about and from which foreclosure is made of them. The real-transcendental identity (of) faith is no longer a species of its unitary form but that which unifies-in-the-last-identity its religious, rationalist, and metaphysical forms. From the originary faith, as philosophy can think it, we extract and experiment on a uni-originary faith by its ultimate human cause and archi-originary in relation to its Christian form. This is the operation of determining or cloning faith but certainly not the operation of its foundation or its divine donation. It is no longer the Principle of Sufficient Faith, it is a procedure non-positional (of) self proper to non-Christianity, with which the Christ-subject constitutes itself as much as he can be constituted. This procedure will serve, with heresy, to model Christianity.

## FROM THE PRINCIPLE OF SUFFICIENT HERESY
## TO NON-GNOSTIC HERESY

Probably from its poorly identifiable origins, gnosis was invested with philosophy and only discernible from it with great difficulty. But we can isolate an evidently unhistorical Gnostic posture, characterized by a triple primacy apparently inverse to that of Christianity, but which absolutely does not reproduce a hierarchy of that type and which it must finish extracting point by point, under the term of 'non-Gnosticism', from philosophy and Christianity joined together.

1.    Primacy of uncreated man, philosophically and theologically unengendered, over God-the-Creator. In order to finish liberating it from ontology, we 'will decide' generally for that Gnostic core, as primacy of the final-identity of Man-in-Man over the onto-theological apparatus, over Being and over God.

2.    Primacy of 'heretical separation' over Christian unity and its own kind of separation with the World, still similar to those of philosophy and ontology by their ecstatic form and transcendence. In order to determine-in-the-last-identity and universalize that heretical posture, rendering it usable as a procedure proper to the Christ-subject, we 'will decide' for that Gnostic core, as primacy of being-Separated, over every act of separation and its modes (creation, crucifixion and resurrection).

3.    Primacy of knowledge over faith. This meaning can be radicalized as primacy of unlearned knowing, immanent or revealed-without-revelation, over faith-in-Christ as expectation and decision and over philosophical or rational faith as 'transcending'. The specific danger in gnosis is here, always by sufficiency, of overestimating or overvaluating the theoretical side and precisely of lapsing in reality into the Greco-philosophical *theoreticism*. If *gnosis* is not reduced to a modern and rational primacy of knowledge as concept or intuition over faith, it is nonetheless marked by intellectualism. As 'faith' is for us now the philosophical symptom of every transcending, 'gnosis' is treated here as the philosophical symptom of the immanent Real.

Understood in its abstraction as a principle, heresy is at any rate a new experience of humanity which has no exact equivalent in other religions. It opposes itself, as non-acquired immanence of a body of knowledge, to the immanence of Life as 'expectation-in-Christ', but above all, first as separation and rejection of the World, against the Christian half-separation proper to the 'creature'. It equally opposes itself to the internal and external philosophical division of identity and to the ontological over-identity. That which it introduces under this form is the initiation of unilateral duality, the being-separated from a term in relation to the All, a term which remains in its particularity and does not become universal or total again. It is already a procedure for a treatment of the World's hegemonic power, but exercised by a still transcendent term, which separates itself without making a hierarchy but instead a duality equal in the allergy, and that affirms its independence by its outside, its dissidence. The experience of a *force of rupture that makes and maintains duality* is an original phenomenon. Heresy makes Two in a completely different manner than philosophy, without preparing a new system or returning to the form of the former. Separation is thus not a 'phenomenological distance' of donation but taking distance from, leaving or a rejection of the World. This is also another way of abandoning the World, in the view of the Christian, to the image of Christ that is itself removed for the Life-in-glory and from which an 'ascension' or 'ascent' separates it. The heretical but classical One joins with Separation by which it dis-identifies Unity, it is without worldly content and has none other than itself and only its being separated, certainly still by transcendence. The two hierarchized transcendences, *meta* and *epekeina*, are necessary to constitute the One-Other of philosophy, they are now cut, reduced to their surface of rejection and co-extensive rather than hierarchized – the ascent to the sky is identical to the rejection of the World. Metaphysical and theological tend to merge. The double articulation of the philosophical system is left broken from that Gnostic adventure, its space is nevertheless that of Two, without doubt filled with mythological imagery which has taken the place of knowledge, itself concentrated elsewhere in men under a form less eidetic and conceptual, more a living experience.

Knowledge (in the Gnostic sense) possesses an aspect of immanence under the form of an already accomplished revelation and even from a *radical revealed*, as a *true-without-truth*. But there is no donation of unity strictly speaking; this is not acquired in-Christ but already given-in-knowledge, in a kind of given-without-givenness. However unity, in religions as in philosophy, is never rigorously given without givenness or really immanent, but at least makes the object of a creation. This is why another authority charged with mitigating its transcendence must support it. As gnosis refuses the donation by the faith-in-Christ of that unity of the living, it must base this on another principle which is the autonomy or reality of Separation. There is also here an order of phenomena, Separation conditions the immanence of knowledge and this grounds the unity of the living as separated from the World. This primacy of Separation shows that heresy which we emphasized in gnosis, as much as it is about freeing a principle, a principle of heresy, rather than that of describing a historical-religious formation. Thus untangled from philosophy and Christianity, reduced to its invariant and minimal posture, heresy can in its turn contribute to modelling Christianity and be determined by cloning as Christ-subject.

## PERFORMING SALVATION

Non-Christianity demands complete modification of the metaphysical technology of classical philosophical distinctions, which are of reciprocity and convertibility, either immediately and explicitly or in the background and from an ultimate horizon (the behind-metaphysics which doubles 'metaphysics' and escapes every criticism and deconstruction). More profoundly there are no longer any decisions or first separations in the sense where they would also have the primacy of the Real. Non-Christianity evidently knows multiple forms of transcendence and decision, but it transforms them in determining their 'priority' by the primacy of Man-in-Man as immanent unilaterity. Finally it experiments on a subject that merges with the clone of Christian faith and the heretical being-separated. The ultimate cause of this mix, and this non-mixture, is Gnostic knowledge, but radicalized. We will avoid opposing faith and knowledge once again.

Non-Christianity undoes the massive unitaries of religions from which the principle of sufficiency expresses itself in the permanent repeating of auto-justification. If it is completely analysed in its composition as phenomena of transcendence, justification by faith or by works is the symptom of a system of auto-justification that is more profound and easily taken up again by philosophy which gives it another meaning. Non-Christianity does not prevent this hetero-justification of faith and knowledge by 'man' but, it is completely different, a determination in-the-last-humanity by the Just. Man-in-Man is the Just-in-person, Christ is the Justified, and it is up to him to justify God-the-World itself.

Modelling Christianity by that double procedure and determining this in-the-last-identify, such is performing salvation. There are some inevitable distinctions needed if we are to understand these formulas. We have found in 'Man-in-person' or still, as we have said, in the 'vision-in-One', the authority which does not need salvation, even less than God-the-World. This is more than a Redeemed-without-redemption, it is *who* gives the reality that is salvation. He who is still bound for salvation, if it is not Man-in-Man, we find it in 'the-man' of the-philosophy and the-religion, enchanted by the World. And *who* is the Salvation-in-person, the Redeemer-already-redeemed, if not that subject who is not Christian but is for Christianity and gnosis, the Future Christ?

### THE MYSTIC PRISM

Non-Christianity makes use of gnosis or Gnostic elements without being a renewed ancient gnosis or one dressed up anew. It uses Christian in the same way and with the same reservations. More exactly, it uses their diverse mixtures measuring the one according to the other. But 'by right' or 'in-Real', it no longer comes under the faith of one or the other. This indifference is how it radicalizes the mystical element of these religions and this indifference, which is susceptible to distinct modes, allows it to be conceived as a unified practice (just not as unitary or syncretistic) of the Judeo-Christian faith and Gnostico-Christian knowledge. The *primacy* of that mystical element over the religious forms and authorities of the faith, inversely, does not exclude the recourse to gnosis and Judaism in their Christian mixture, and even frees, as it is visible, the *priority* sometimes of the one and sometimes of the other. The mystical indifference, the constitutive non-consistency of Man-in-person, is that which we oppose to the mortifying violence of the churches, to Christianity in the measure where immediately it pronounces itself as ecclesiological sufficiency and partially as Verb-logos. Opposed also to gnosis in the measure where, a victim of the churches, it is also a victim of resentment and refuses to be-for-the-World. Finally, it is almost pointless to add, to all the forms of sectarian and religious terrorism.

With the mystical indifference, the exposition of the problem's facts arrives at its maturity. Rather than taking at random religious material, according to this or that conjuncture of faith and thought, we centre on this relationship of Christianity, gnosis and the inevitable philosophy in a particularly concentrated material, in the prism of Christian mysticism. Non-philosophy in general tolerates a contingent and conjectural diversity of materials, even Christianity and gnosis in their generality could have provided extraordinarily varied data. But Christian mysticism, it also being a unitary, idealized and mixed formation, here makes a law and so we give up justifying our choice of material, despite being rather traditional. It holds over every other the certain advantage of realizing, at least by right if not in a historical and factual manner, the asymptomatic coincidence of faith, philosophy (under a form above all neo-Platonic) and heresy. Mysticism is like a heresy on the inside margin of Christianity which it tolerates as an expression of faith rather than as a theology, while 'the' heresies properly so called developed on the outside theological margins. We know that the Church barely hesitated to denounce them using appropriate restraints. But this is not about a pardon eventually requested by the Church for the mystics and heretics that we need; this is about the non-Christian strength of untying from the churches the universal human, of snatching him from his claimed *being-in-the-Church* or *from the Principle of Sufficient Church*.

It is within this mystic field that we will test the terms and new problems by the means of the non-Christian programme. Hence 'mystical theorems' distinct from neo-Platonic 'theorems', which are in reality more theoreticist than theoretical in a quasi-scientific sense, and more transcendental in an ontological sense than non-philosophical. 'Non-Christian science' draws on the materiality of its axioms and those of its theorems in the religion-world but distinguishes in a unilateral manner the former and the latter by their theoretical status either by symbolized and formalized premises, or by theorems transcendentally concluded in the occasion of the experience of the religion-world. The mystical theorems form the living content of the new non-Christian experience, in some way the radical living experience of salvation of the Future Christ.

# Other works by François Laruelle

PHILOSOPHY I

*Phénomène et différence. Essai sur Ravaisson* (Paris: Klincksieck, 1971)
*Machines textuelles. Déconstruction et libido-d'écriture* (Paris: Le Seuil, 1976)
*Nietzsche contre Heidegger* (Paris: Payot, 1977)
*Le déclin de l'écriture* (Paris: Aubier-Flammarion, 1977)
*Au-delà de principe de pouvoir* (Paris: Payot, 1978)


PHILOSOPHY II

*Le principe de minorité* (Paris: Aubier, 1981)
*Unebiographie de l'homme ordinaire. Des autorités et minorités* (Paris: Aubier, 1985)
*Philosophies of Difference: A Critical Introduction to Non-Philosophy*, trans. Rocco Gangle (New York and London: Continuum, 2010 [1987])
*Philosophie et non-philosophie* (Liège-Bruxelles: Mardaga, 1989)
*En tant qu'Un* (Paris: Aubier, 1991)
*Théorie des identités* (Paris: PUF, 1992)


PHILOSOPHY III

*Théorie des Étrangers* (Paris: Kimé, 1995)
*Principes de la non-philosophie* (Paris: PUF, 1995)

**OTHER WORKS BY FRANÇOIS LARUELLE**

*Éthique de l'Étranger* (Paris: Kimé, 2000)
*Introduction au non-marxisme* (Paris: PUF, 2000)


PHILOSOPHY IV

*Future Christ: A Lesson in Heresy*, trans. Anthony Paul Smith (New York
    and London: Continuum, 2010 [2002])
*L'ultime honneur des intellectuels* (Paris: Textuel, 2003)
*La Lutte et l'Utopie à la fin des temps philosophiques* (Paris: Kimé, 2004)
*Mystique non-philosophique à l'usage des contemporains* (Paris: L'Harmattan,
    2007)


PHILOSOPHY V

*Introduction aux sciences génériques* (Paris: Petra, 2008)

# Index